The Sino-Vietnamese
Territorial Dispute

THE WASHINGTON PAPERS

... intended to meet the need for an authoritative, yet prompt, public appraisal of the major developments in world affairs.

Series Editors: Walter Laqueur; Amos A. Jordan

Associate Editors: William J. Taylor, Jr.; M. Jon Vondracek

Executive Editor: Jean C. Newsom

Managing Editor: Nancy B. Eddy

Editorial Assistant: Ann E. Ellsworth

MANUSCRIPT SUBMISSION

The Washington Papers and Praeger Publishers welcome inquiries concerning manuscript submissions. Please include with your inquiry a curriculum vita, synopsis, table of contents, and estimated manuscript length. Submissions to *The Washington Papers* should be sent to *The Washington Papers*; The Center for Strategic and International Studies; Georgetown University; 1800 K Street NW; Suite 400; Washington, DC 20006. Book proposals should be sent to Praeger Publishers; 521 Fifth Avenue; New York NY 10175.

ACKNOWLEDGMENT

The author wishes to express his gratitude to the publisher of the *Asia Pacific Community* for its permission to incorporate materials that have appeared earlier in that journal.

The Sino-Vietnamese Territorial Dispute

Pao-min Chang

Foreword by Douglas Pike

Published with The Center for
Strategic and International Studies,
Georgetown University, Washington, D.C.

PRAEGER SPECIAL STUDIES • PRAEGER SCIENTIFIC

New York • Philadelphia • Eastbourne, UK
Toronto • Hong Kong • Tokyo • Sydney

Library of Congress Cataloging in Publication Data

Chang, Pao-min.
  The Sino-Vietnamese territorial dispute.

  (The Washington papers, ISSN 0278-937X ; Vol XIII, 118)
  "Published with the Center for Strategic Studies,
Georgetown University, Washington, D.C."
  Includes bibliographical references.
  1. Sino-Vietnamese Conflict, 1979.   I. Title.
II. Series.
DS559.916.C43   1985   959.704′4   85-19445
ISBN 0-03-007233-6
ISBN 0-03-007232-8 (pbk.)

Published in 1986 by Praeger Publishers
CBS Educational and Professional Publishing, a Division of CBS Inc.
521 Fifth Avenue, New York, NY 10175 USA

© 1986 by The Center for Strategic and International Studies

Printed in the United States of America on acid-free paper

INTERNATIONAL OFFICES

Orders from outside the United States should be sent to the appropriate address listed below. Orders from
areas not listed below should be placed through CBS International Publishing, 383 Madison Ave., New York,
NY 10175 USA

Australia, New Zealand
Holt Saunders, Pty, Ltd., 9 Waltham St., Artarmon, N.S.W. 2064, Sydney, Australia
Canada
Holt, Rinehart & Winston of Canada, 55 Horner Ave., Toronto, Ontario, Canada M8Z 4X6
Europe, the Middle East, & Africa
Holt Saunders, Ltd., 1 St. Anne's Road, Eastbourne, East Sussex, England BN21 3UN
Japan
Holt Saunders, Ltd., Ichibancho Central Building, 22-1 Ichibancho, 3rd Floor, Chiyodaku, Tokyo, Japan
Hong Kong, Southeast Asia
Holt Saunders Asia, Ltd., 10 Fl, Intercontinental Plaza, 94 Granville Road, Tsim Sha Tsui East, Kowloon,
Hong Kong

Manuscript submissions should be sent to the Editorial Director, Praeger Publishers, 521 Fifth Avenue, New
York, NY 10175 USA

Published and Distributed by the
Praeger Publishers Division
(ISBN Prefix 0-275)
of Greenwood Press, Inc.,
Westport, Connecticut

Contents

Foreword

Pao-min Chang is a political scientist and scholar at the National University in Singapore, trained in the United States and Taiwan, who has in recent years written extensively on the sources of conflict between those two ancient rivals whose disputations are hoary with age: China and Vietnam. He has written on their dispute over Kampuchea, about their quarrel over Hanoi's mistreatment of ethnic Chinese in Vietnam, about their brief 1979 border war, and, here, about their several territorial disputes. In the course of this writing, Pao-min Chang has become an authority on the subject of Sino-Vietnamese contention.

The general history of the relationship between the Chinese and the Vietnamese is a long and complicated one. By comparison, the Soviet-Vietnamese relationship is elemental and of only recent origin. For millennia the Vietnamese and Chinese have lived side by side intimately, sometimes in harmony, more often in struggle. During this association through the centuries, the Vietnamese borrowed heavily from China – law, architecture, culture – virtually an entire civilization, although the Vietnamese are reluctant to admit this even to themselves. Living in such close association for so long, with cultural and sociopolitical institutions so similar, has produced an inevitable result, an extraordinarily close relation, more marriage than neighbor. And because of this, on both sides, there has developed a set of highly complex attitudes and what in psychological terms would be termed a love-hate relationship. The relation then is complex, symbiotic, and volatile and is destined to so remain.

In this work, Pao-min Chang addresses himself to the territorial disputes between the two countries. Some of these are insular, involving the 800-mile border that runs through spiney mountains down to the sea. Some are maritime, quarrels over those dots of land in the South China sea that in earlier centuries Chinese sailors called the Isles of Dangerous Places.

Territorial disputes are, of course, commonplace among nations and, it seems, almost always intractable, enduring, and likely to arouse unreasoned national sentiment even though they are over bits of real estate that in other circumstances neither would probably care the least about. Sino-Vietnamese territorial disputes are now encrusted with age with some of the claims dating back into the mists of antiquity. The claims are further complicated because of the dubious evidence often submitted on both sides: maps produced by French colonialists, papers from the Vietnamese Court at Hue, records of Imperial China, all of which at the time had their own interests to serve. Whatever else, however, these disputes are durable. We can count on them to continue to plague the relationship between the two countries long after many of the present issues standing between them have faded into history.

Pao-min Chang has done a masterful job in tracing these disputes through the years and in and out of the arena of contending and often convoluted claims. The reader will find his study interesting, informative, and important.

Douglas Pike
Indochina Studies Project
Institute of East Asian Studies
University of California, Berkeley

About the Author

Dr. Pao-min Chang is a senior lecturer in the Department of Political Science at the National University of Singapore. He holds a Ph.D. in political science from Brown University and an M.A. from Southern Illinois University. He did his undergraduate work at Tunghai University in Taiwan. Dr. Chang has published extensively on China and Vietnam, including *Beijing, Hanoi, and the Overseas Chinese* (Institute of East Asian Studies, University of California, Berkeley) and *Kampuchea between China and Vietnam* (Singapore University Press).

Introduction

Perhaps the least expected and most dramatic development in Southeast Asia after the end of the Vietnam War in 1975 was the abrupt and rapid deterioration of relations between the People's Republic of China (PRC) and Vietnam, two former allies once firmly united for the 30 years of the Indochina War. Starting with a marked cooling of ties in 1975, the schism widened in early 1978 into open accusations and counteraccusations and a massive exodus of Chinese residents from Vietnam. By early 1979, the two countries were at war to resolve their disputes, and since then, the prospect of normalizing their relations has remained dim.

What could have turned these two onetime comrades-in-arms into sworn enemies in such a short period? It is impossible to provide a complete explanation for such a complex subject without examining the broader geopolitical rivalry between China and the Soviet Union in Asia and without looking into the recurrent outbursts of animosity that have characterized the uneasy relationship between China and Vietnam for centuries. Three major issues—the controversy over the ethnic Chinese, the territorial dispute, and the war in Kampuchea—have contributed directly to the Sino-Vietamese conflict. Although closely related to one another and mutually reinforcing in effect, the three issues have their distinct origins and characteristics and therefore deserve to be treated separately. Because this paper is devoted to the territorial dispute only, it is useful to summarize briefly the two other areas of conflict, which I have examined in detail elsewhere, to place the entire conflict in its proper perspective.*

The controversy over Chinese residents in Vietnam centered on the issue of assimilation and concerned the presence of at least 1.5 million ethnic Chinese whose economic power was enormous and yet whose political loyalty was divided between Vietnam and China. The problem confronting Hanoi was compounded not only by the geographical contiguity of the two countries and the tremendous Chinese cultural influence in Vietnam throughout its history, but also by the close relationship forged between the two through 30 years of war. Consequently, whereas China could not afford to disregard how the Chinese in Vietnam were treated, Vietnam was always sensitive to any sign of Chinese interference in Vietnam's internal affairs. As long as Vietnam remained China's vassal or close ally, however, the ethnic Chinese in Vietnam were a useful lubricant in the relations between them, and it was politically wise for Vietnam to treat the Chinese well. But once tension developed between China and Vietnam and when Vietnam decided to move away from China, the large Chinese community inevitably became the major object of suspicion and the target of political assault, which in turn further exacerbated the relations between the two nations.

Although the ethnic dispute had many historical antecedents, the seeds of the most recent controversy were sown in 1955 when China and Vietnam reached an ambiguous agreement, according to which ethnic Chinese in the north

---

*For a detailed account of the ideas and information presented in the remaining pages of this chapter, see my *Beijing, Hanoi, and the Overseas Chinese* (Berkeley, Calif.: Institute of East Asian Studies, 1982) and *Kampuchea Between China and Vietnam* (Singapore: Singapore University Press, 1985).

might be naturalized on a voluntary basis and after "sustained and patient persuasion and ideological education." As for the Chinese in the south, the question of their nationality would be solved through consultation between the two countries after Vietnam's liberation. In the ensuing two decades, the Hanoi regime did succeed more or less in integrating the 250 thousand Chinese residing in the north through a series of positive measures. A similar Vietnamization program undertaken by Saigon in the south in the late 1950s backfired miserably, however, not only because of its harsh and drastic nature, but also because of the large number of Chinese — nearly 1.25 million — involved.

Thus, in 1975, when South Vietnam fell to the Communists, Hanoi still faced the enormous problem of integrating more than 1 million urbanized, bourgeois Chinese, whose pro-China sentiments were now openly displayed and whose grip over the south's economy was still unshakable. Clearly motivated by both political and economic considerations, the government decided to speed up the dual process of Vietnamization and socialist transformation by adopting a series of measures aimed against the Chinese in both their occupations and their cultural activities. By the end of 1976, not only were all Chinese newspapers and Chinese language schools closed, but also the pro-China faction in the top party leadership circles was purged. In February 1977, the situation deteriorated further as tens of thousands of Chinese whose loyalty was in doubt were summarily fired from their jobs, with their right of residence revoked and their food rations terminated. The decision had already been made to expel distrusted Chinese, who were required to fill out a form of "voluntary repatriation," and in the spring of 1977, the Chinese residing in the Sino-Vietnamese border areas began to be expelled to China.

All these developments clearly alarmed China, which felt that Vietnam had returned China's decades of unswerving support and sacrifices for Vietnam with blatant ingratitude. After several fruitless rounds of representations had been made to the Vietnamese government at lower levels, Chinese

Vice Premier Li Xiannian brought up the issue directly for the first time in his June 1977 talks with the visiting Vietnamese Premier Pham Van Dong and reminded Dong of the 1955 agreement that forbade the forced naturalization of and discrimination against the Chinese. But no concrete results came of these exchanges. With the border conflict between Vietnam and Kampuchea steadily worsening in the second half of 1977 and with Beijing becoming increasingly sympathetic toward Phnom Penh, the anti-Chinese campaign in Vietnam intensified and resulted in widespread physical harassment of the Chinese and the forcible seizure of their properties. In January 1978, China finally openly expressed its concern about the situation. Beijing also declared its intention not only to "protect the legitimate rights and interests" of all overseas Chinese but also to welcome and make proper arrangements for those who wished to return to China to help with China's modernization.

But such gestures of open support for the Chinese in Vietnam merely provided Hanoi with the final pretext for clamping down on all "bourgeois" activities in the country in March and April of 1978. In a massive operation affecting not only Ho Chi Minh City but also many other cities and causing much violence, raid squads were dispatched to search every shop and house and to confiscate goods. A ban was also proclaimed on all private trade, forcing thousands of wholesale and retail traders out of business overnight. Urban traders stripped of their businesses and properties were ordered to move to the New Economic Zones set up in remote border provinces to reclaim virgin land. The able-bodied were drafted into the armed forces and sent to the Kampuchean-Vietnamese border to fight. Under these circumstances, the refugee flow across the Sino-Vietnamese border quickly turned into an exodus in the spring of 1978, with more than 70 thousand Chinese crossing the land border into China in April and May alone. By the end of July, the number of Chinese entering China already exceeded 160 thousand. Meanwhile, the exodus by sea picked up momentum, and, by the end of August, there were already 30 thousand boat refugees in other Southeast Asian countries.

In the ensuing verbal war, China accused Vietnam of premeditation in "ostracizing, persecuting, and expelling" the Chinese in open violation of the 1955 agreement and held Vietnam responsible for the consequences of the mass exodus. Vietnam retorted by arguing that there were no Chinese nationals in Vietnam, only Vietnamese of Chinese origin, as the question of citizenship had long been settled by previous Vietnamese regimes. It was China that had "deceived, instigated, threatened, and coerced" these Vietnamese of Chinese origin to leave Vietnam.

Tension reached a new high in early June when China decided to send two passenger ships to Vietnam to bring victimized Chinese back to China for repatriation. But Vietnam's reluctance to cooperate in any aspect of the Chinese undertaking caused the entire rescue operation to be cancelled after 19 unsuccessful "urgent meetings" initiated by China at the consular level in Hanoi during June and July. In late July, China again proposed a new round of negotiations, this time at the vice foreign minister's level, to reach an overall solution of the crisis. But throughout the eight sessions, which began in early August and ended in late September, Hanoi insisted on its exclusive right to handle the problem of its citizens and denied China's charges of persecution and expulsion. Consequently, the two sides failed to reach any agreement even on matters of principle, let alone on any substantive issues.

While the talks were stalemated, the exodus of refugees into China continued unabated. By the end of 1978, 200 thousand Chinese either fled or were pushed across the border. The futile negotiations, the endless flow of people, and the sheer chaos that prevailed along the land border finally led China to resort to large-scale military action in February 1979 to retaliate against Vietnam's policy of expulsion and end the refugee crisis.

The Chinese invasion, however, merely made Vietnam all the more determined to expel the entire Chinese population, who now clearly constituted a serious security risk for Hanoi. The open conflict between China and Vietnam also caused widespread panic among the Chinese in Vietnam.

These factors thus combined to produce the largest exodus in modern history, and the blocking of land routes merely led to a massive flow by sea immediately following the February border war. During 1979 alone, as many as 200 thousand boat refugees managed to reach the shores of other Southeast Asian countries. Another 50 thousand land refugees joined those already in China, in spite of all the precautionary measures China had taken to stem the flow. Although China raised the issue again during the peace talks following the border war, Vietnam was determined to allow the exodus to complete its natural course. By the end of 1980, the total number of land refugees in China had exceeded 260 thousand — the equivalent of the entire Chinese population in the north. At the same time, the total number of boat people had risen to 400 thousand. Assuming conservatively that one out of every two boat refugees survived in the harsh, unpredictable sea journey, the totals indicate that the entire Chinese population in the south could well have also been all but completely eliminated. The ethnic dispute thus ended in a most bizarre and tragic way for the Chinese in Vietnam.

If the ethnic dispute involved essentially a domestic issue with international implications, the conflict between Vietnam and China over Kampuchea was rooted in a basic clash over the perceptions of Kampuchea's status in Indochina, as well as in the conflicting security needs of Kampuchea and Vietnam. Historically, Kampuchea was marginal to China's political concerns because of geographical distance and vast cultural differences, and China always considered it an independent nation with unique features. Vietnam, however, saw its own destiny closely tied with that of Kampuchea as a result of a centuries-old suzerainty relationship, reinforced by Vietnam's dominant role in the prolonged anticolonial and anti-imperialist struggle throughout Indochina. If the Vietnamese were from time to time suspicious of growing Chinese influence in Vietnam, the Khmers of Kampuchea were always undisguised in their resentment of Vietnamese paternalism. The triangular relationship was completed by Kampuchea's age-old strategy of using outside powers as a counterweight to Vietnam in order to ensure Kampuchea's physical survival and by China's interest in at least preventing Indochina from becoming hostile to China.

Chinese and Vietnamese divergent perceptions of and policies toward Kampuchea can be traced back recently to the 1954 Geneva Conference, during which China, as well as the Soviet Union, pressured Vietnam to withdraw its guerrilla forces completely from Kampuchea as a condition of the peace settlement, in spite of the well-entrenched Vietnamese presence in the country. During the ensuing decade and a half, a close relationship was forged between China and Kampuchea as a result of Beijing's drive to neutralize the growing U.S. presence in Indochina and of Kampuchea's desire to reduce the might of a United States allied with both of Kampuchea's two distrusted neighbors. From Kampuchea's viewpoint, to be confronted by one hostile neighbor already constituted a serious problem. This de facto alliance reinforced China's commitment to an independent Kampuchea, and indeed Beijing never hesitated to articulate this commitment in public, much to the chagrin of Hanoi.

Hanoi's stance on Kampuchea during the same period was characterized by a consistent ambivalence toward Kampuchea's legal status, as shown by Hanoi's reluctance to endorse the existing borders of Kampuchea or to support Prince Norodom Sihanouk's repeated proposals for an international guarantee of Kampuchea's independence, which only heightened Kampuchea's traditional suspicions. In fact, tension developed in the late 1960s when North Vietnam firmly reestablished its military presence in Kampuchea as the insurgency in South Vietnam intensified. Particularly after the 1970 rightist coup d'etat against Prince Sihanouk, Hanoi sought to expand further its political influence in Kampuchea. The five years of 1970 to 1975 therefore witnessed intensive behind-the-scene maneuvering by all three parties in the precarious triangular alliance, with Hanoi attempting to regain its dominant position in the Khmer revolution, the Khmers playing China off against Vietnam, and China striving to preserve both a united front and the separate identity of Kampuchea.

The turning point came in 1975 with the Communist victory in both Vietnam and Kampuchea, which quickly revived the old aspirations of Vietnam and the old fears of Kampuchea, thereby forcing China to tilt in favor of the relatively weaker Kampuchea. Having provided the crucial support to Phnom Penh during the war years, Hanoi felt entitled to a special honorific status in Kampuchea and demanded close policy coordination between the two. Because Kampuchea had historically been the victim of Vietnamese territorial aggrandizement and cultural inroads and it was now confronted with pervasive Vietnamese influence, the new Khmer regime saw the Vietnamese initiatives as no more than thinly veiled ruses to dominate Kampuchea. Partly blinded by conceit and partly eager to keep Vietnam at bay, the new Phnom Penh regime, once set up, adopted a vehemently anti-Vietnamese stance and proceeded to carry out extensive purges within all sectors of Kampuchea's power structure and to expel Vietnamese nationals en masse. By late 1975, a border war was under way between Kampuchea and Vietnam.

Although Kampuchea's hostility toward Vietnam was neither engineered nor approved by China, Beijing's long-standing friendship with Phnom Penh and the massive aid China continued to pour into Kampuchea after 1975 constituted sufficient proof to Hanoi of China's culpability in Kampuchea's anti-Vietnam policy. As it could not tolerate a hostile Kampuchea backed by an outside power, Hanoi decided to enlist Soviet assistance to counterbalance the Chinese presence, which only generated new anxieties in Beijing about the extent of Vietnam's regional ambitions. The result was a rapid realignment of forces in Indochina. Whether it was China's sympathy for Kampuchea that triggered Vietnam's campaign against the Chinese community in Vietnam or Vietnam's anti-Chinese campaign that alerted China to Vietnam's ulterior motives in Indochina, the two issues were seen by both sides as closely linked, thereby further poisoning their relations.

In the course of 1977, Phnom Penh launched a series of attacks into Vietnamese territory, which were seen by Hanoi as clearly Chinese-inspired. The series of Vietnamese counteroffensives against Kampuchea, particularly toward the end of 1977, were considered by China as a blatant bullying of a smaller country with Soviet endorsement. In early 1978, China finally came out openly in support of Kampuchea and sent it large amounts of arms. Throughout the spring and summer of 1978, Hanoi accused China of sowing dissension among the three Indochinese peoples, "sabotaging the tradition of solidarity and friendship between Vietnam and Kampuchea," and using Kampuchea's Pol Pot regime as an instrument to weaken Vietnam and conquer Southeast Asia. China, on the other hand, accused Vietnam of waging "a naked war of aggression against Kampuchea" and of seeking to establish an Indochina federation with Hanoi at its head. Beijing also identified Hanoi's pursuit of hegemonism as the underlying cause of Vietnam's anti-China stance and activities.

As Vietnam tilted increasingly toward the Soviet Union and also increased its military pressure on Kampuchea as the only way of achieving its goals in Indochina, China was left with no choice but to move even closer to Kampuchea, if only to curb the growing Soviet-Vietnamese threat from Indochina. The conclusion of the Soviet-Vietnamese Friendship Treaty in November 1978 finally provided Vietnam with the necessary political backing to attempt a quick military victory over Kampuchea. But the Vietnamese invasion of China's ally, launched in December 1978, turned out to be too humiliating a blow to China's stature and credibility for Beijing to stand idly by. The prospect of Soviet penetration in China's southern flank also compelled Beijing to rush to Kampuchea's rescue. Thus China's invasion of Vietnam in February 1979 was explicitly linked to the situation in Kampuchea.

Far from altering Vietnam's objectives in Kampuchea, however, the Chinese invasion supplied Vietnam with its hitherto clearest evidence of Beijing's collusion with Phnom Penh. As such, it provided Hanoi with both the pretext and the need to continue its occupation of Kampuchea. On the other hand, the Chinese invasion, being a most forceful demonstration of China's protest over Vietnam's Kampuchea policy, inextricably entangled China with the cause of the Khmer resistance. The peace talks held between China and Vietnam after the 1979 border war thus saw the two parties as adamant as ever, with Beijing demanding that Vietnam withdraw completely from Kampuchea and Hanoi demanding that China stop threatening Vietnam through Kampuchea, as their respective preconditions of a peaceful settlement. The years since the border war have seen China openly and consistently championing the cause of an independent, neutral Kampuchea and Vietnam telling the world unequivocably and repeatedly that the issue was closed and the situation in Kampuchea was irreversible. In the meantime, almost every large-scale Vietnamese offensive against the Khmer forces has led to increased Chinese military pressure along the Sino-Vietnamese land border. Because China is as determined to support the Khmer resistance movement as Vietnam is confident of obtaining a final victory, the conflict is far from over.

Compared with the ethnic dispute and the war in Kampuchea, the territorial dispute may appear to be the least dramatic cause of the Sino-Vietnamese conflict, but it is by no means less important. In fact, the territorial dispute also had its own historical antecedents and was the first public area of controversy between the two countries. As such, it definitely has had a direct impact on the development of the other disputes and the overall course of the bilateral conflict. Because of its extensive scope and far-reaching implications for the other states in the region, the territorial dispute certainly will remain the last dispute to be resolved between Hanoi and Beijing. What then is the nature of the dispute? How has it evolved? What are the problems and the prospect for a peaceful settlement in the foreseeable future? This paper analyzes and answers some of these questions.

1

Origins of the Dispute

The territorial dispute between China and Vietnam centers around three main issues, each with its own distinct origin and unique problems. They are the 797-mile long land border separating northern Vietnam from China's Guangdong, Guangxi, and Yunnan Provinces; the Gulf of Tonkin enclosed by the northern Vietnamese coast and the Chinese island of Hainan; and two offshore island groups in the South China Sea, namely the Spratlies and the Paracels.

The Sino-Vietnamese land border was demarcated in 1887 as a result of the Sino-French War of 1884–1885, which led to the placement of Indochina under French protection. Generally speaking, the border is more clearly delimited than in the case of Sino-Indian or Sino-Soviet borders because of its relatively short length and because easily identifiable rivers constitute nearly one-third of the boundary. Although it took 11 years to delineate the boundary, not without much hard bargaining and diplomatic tussles, final agreement was reached by 1895 with the conclusion of at least six separate conventions, and 333 markers were erected to indicate the boundary.[1]

As with other treaties on territorial matters concluded between China and other countries in the nineteenth century, however, the Sino-French boundary conventions were not always clear in language nor consistent in their references and implications. Because the entire boundary runs through mountainous terrain and the border areas have been traditionally inhabited by large numbers of non-Chinese and non-Vietnamese minority groups, with much cross-border activity, division of actual administrative responsibilities also has not been always easy or clear.[2] Moreover, throughout the late nineteenth century and the first half of the twentieth century, because of the prevalence of a weak central government and prolonged civil disorder in China, many places lying north of the Sino-French boundary fell under de facto French jurisdiction; some of the land markers were also destroyed by forces of nature during the same period, thereby blurring the boundary line in some other places. As a matter of record, Chinese official documents of the Qing Dynasty, including memorials submitted to the emperor, are replete with accounts of the loss of scattered pieces of Chinese territory to the French after 1896 and the damage done to boundary markers by natural forces.[3]

After 1949, the Chinese government more or less acquiesced in this de facto situation, apparently in recognition of the continuing turmoil in the entire region.[4] With the onset of the first Indochina War in 1946 and particularly the second Indochina War in 1954, local Chinese authorities also helped the Vietnamese with the administration of certain places in the border areas, apparently for strategic and logistical purposes during the drawn-out conflict, if not also to relieve Vietnam of unnecessary financial burdens during its darkest years.[5]

The territories affected by all these circumstances have not been substantial in size or number, however. According to Vietnam, China has occupied areas ranging from 100 meters to a few kilometers inside Vietnamese territory.[6] According to China, no more than 60 square kilometers are involved, and these areas are scattered over the entire land border.[7] Nevertheless, it can be difficult to agree on a common line after such a long lapse of time. The controversy is essentially over whether the Sino-French boundary accords should remain the only valid legal basis for demarcation of the border or whether the actual state of affairs brought about by historical factors should also constitute a valid basis for making territorial claims.

The issue of the Gulf of Tonkin (Beibu Gulf to China and Bac Bo Gulf to Vietnam) concerns the division of the water area of the entire gulf. The dispute originates not from the administrative changes taking place after the Sino-French War, however, but from the ambiguity of the boundary accords as a result of the discrepancy between the Chinese and French texts of the relevant treaty provisions. The 1887 Sino-French Convention on the boundary between Annam (Vietnam) and China's Guangdong Province made an implicit reference to the gulf by drawing a straight red line on relevant maps extending from the eastern end of the Sino-Vietnamese land border southward into the gulf. Although the Convention specifically states that islands located to the east of this line belong to China and islands lying west of it belong to Annam, there are apparent discrepancies between the Chinese and French versions of the Convention as to whether the line divides only the islands or whether it separates the water area as well. Whereas the Chinese text is quite clear that the red line applies "so far as the islands in the sea are concerned," the French text defines the red line as coinciding with 108 degrees and 3 minutes 13 seconds east of the Greenwich meridian and "as making up the frontier" between China and Annam. Because this provision is the single most crucial source of controversy with far-reaching implications, the English translations of its two versions are given as follows:[8]

1. The Chinese version: *As far as the islands in the sea are concerned* [italics added], the red line drawn by the officials of the two countries responsible for delineating the boundary shall be extended southward from the eastern hilltop of Chagushe [or *Wanzhu* in Chinese] and constitutes the dividing line. The islands lying east of this line shall belong to China. The island of Jiutousan (*Gotho* in Vietnamese) and other small islands west of this line shall belong to Vietnam.

2. The French version: The islands east of the meridian 105°43′ east of the Paris meridian [i.e., the meridian 108°03′ 18″ east of the Greenwich meridian], that is, east of the north-south line passing through the eastern tip of the Tch'a-kou or Ouan-chan (Tra-co) and *forming the boundary* [italics added], are all assigned to China. The Gotho islands and other islands lying west of that meridian belong to Annam.

No mention was made in either text as to where this red line should end. To extend it all the way down would cut through part of Vietnam, which was clearly not intended by the treaty. To terminate it at the Vietnamese coast would confine its applicability to the gulf, or, in a more liberal sense, to the entire sea area off Vietnam. One interpretation of the provisions of the Convention would make the red line the sea boundary between China and Vietnam, which would give Vietnam control over the greater portion of the gulf. Another interpretation, which conforms to existing international law of the sea governing gulfs, would regard the line as nothing more than demarcating the islands in the sea, thereby leaving the gulf as high seas open to free international traffic except for a strip of territorial waters contiguous to the coasts.[9] Because there is no specific mention in the entire Convention of the gulf as such, the second interpretation also allows one to apply the red line to all the islands in the seas off Vietnam. The dispute therefore is essentially one over the interpretations of treaty terms. (See map 1.)

But the most complex and better known issue of conflict concerns the sovereignty over the Paracels and the Spratlies (*Xisha* and *Nansha* in Chinese, and *Hoana Sa* and *Truong Sa* in Vietnamese), which are not explicitly governed by the Sino-French boundary accords. These two archipelagoes comprise more than 150 tiny and often barren islets, reefs, and sandbanks invariably smaller than one square mile each and spread over a sea area of more than 200 thousand square miles. Whereas the strategic value of these two island groups is obvious enough because of their control over the main sea-lanes between the Indian Ocean and the Pacific, they have attracted new attention since the late 1960s when these areas

MAP 1. The Land Border & the Gulf of Tonkin

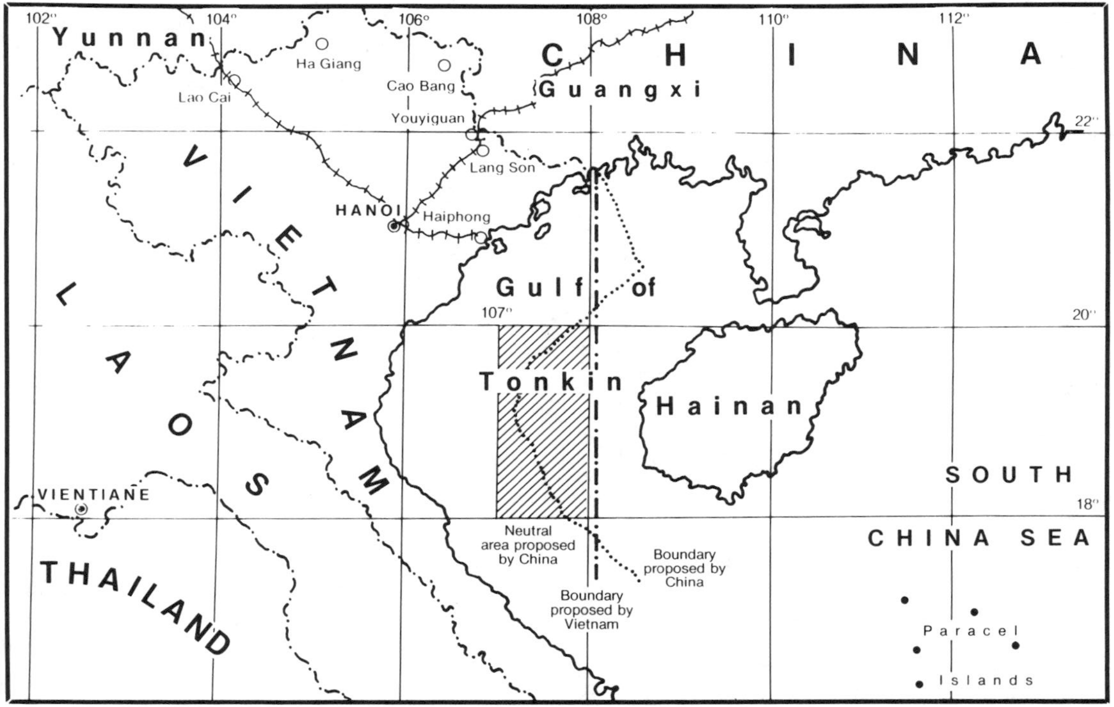

became known as rich in undersea oil deposits.[10] According to the prevailing principles of the law of the sea, any coastal state with a valid legal title to these archipelagoes presumably would be able to have almost the entire South China Sea as its exclusive economic zone, as China has customarily indicated on all its maps.[11]

As far as sovereignty is concerned, however, these islands do not form the natural geographical extensions of any land mass and therefore are not readily a part of any coastal state. In fact, precisely because of the vast expanse of sea encompassed by the islands and the difficulty of establishing any form of permanent settlement on them, no country — neither China nor Vietnam nor France before Vietnam became independent — could claim effective occupation over the whole of either archipelago for any sustained period at any time in history. Between 1701 and 1883, Dutch, French, and German ships passed through or stopped over, and some even made surveys and designated names as if discovering them for the first time. The Europeans made no attempt to settle, however.[12]

China is probably the first country to have discovered the islands, as is evident from the many cultural relics found, and Chinese fishermen started exploiting them as early as the third century B.C. and used them as resting places throughout later centuries. The Chinese government failed to claim formal sovereignty over them until 1909, however, when the Paracels were incorporated into Guangdong Province. In the same year, three Chinese warships were sent to the Paracels to conduct a comprehensive survey. A Chinese flag was hoisted on the main island and a stone landmark erected. Landmarks were erected again by the Chinese in 1912, 1921, 1926, and 1927.[13] But apart from these symbolic acts, no effective occupation or permanent settlement was attempted during these decades. As a result, the actual control of these islands has changed hands at least three times.

In 1932, France made the first open challenge to the Chinese claim by citing evidence that the kingdom of Annam was the first to establish formal sovereignty over the Paracels, in 1816, and a map entitled *Geography of Vietnam* (*Hoang-Viet Dea-Du*) published in 1835 already included these islands as part of Annam.[14] China immediately retorted by pointing out that before 1875 Vietnam was still a Chinese protectorate and as such could not have possibly annexed Chinese territory.[15] In a memorandum sent to the French government in September 1932, China argued that both archipelagoes lay to the east of the red line specified in the 1887 boundary convention and that the line applied to all islands in the sea.[16] When diplomatic correspondence failed to resolve the differences between the two countries, France in 1933 proceeded to seize control of the nine main islands in the Spratly group over Chinese protests and in 1937 took over the entire Paracels group while China was tied down by its war with Japan.

But the French domination of these islands was short lived. In February 1939, as Japan moved into Southeast Asia, both island groups fell to the Japanese and were incorporated into the then Japanese-occupied Taiwan. Almost immediately after the end of World War II, both China and France reiterated their claims to both island groups, and, in November 1946, China dispatched four warships to take over the Pratas, the Paracels, and the Spratlies from the defeated Japanese. Official ceremonies were held and sovereignty markers erected on all the three archipelagoes. Four main islands in the Paracels and the Spratlies were then renamed after the visiting warships, and a small garrison was established on the largest island in each of these archipelagoes.[17] These measures were followed by the official promulgation of the Chinese names of all the islands China claimed in the South China Sea on December 1, 1947 and their incorporation under Hainan Island in April 1949.[18] During 1945–1946, France also repeatedly sent warships to the Paracels and the Spratlies and in November 1946 even seized Robert Island in the Paracels for a short while and set up a meteorological station in spite of China's protest.[19] No attempt was made to effect any form of permanent occupation, however.

In 1948, with the onset of the first Indochina War,

France withdrew completely from both island groups. The evacuation of the Chinese Nationalist troops stationed on the Paracels followed in 1950 as a result of their defeat in the civil war in China. Although Chinese civilians soon moved into a few Paracel islands and an administrative office was set up in March 1959, a small contingent of Taiwanese troops remained on the largest island — *Itu Aba* (Taiping) — in the Spratly group, and Taipei also retained control of the Pratas.[20] With no Chinese troops on the Paracels and virtually no one on most of the Spratly islands, a power vacuum existed in the two archipelagoes throughout the 1950s and 1960s. The new regime in Beijing, however, did claim sovereignty over all these islands as early as August 15, 1951, when Chinese Foreign Minister Zhou Enlai, in a statement on the draft peace treaty proposed by the Allies to Japan, declared that the islands in the South China Sea, including the Paracels and the Spratlies, "have always been China's territory. Although they were occupied by Japan for some time during the war of aggression waged by Japanese imperialism, they were all taken over by the then Chinese government following Japan's surrender."[21] Similarly, in September 1951, at the San Francisco Conference from which both China and Taiwan were excluded, Vietnam "confirmed the sovereignty over the Hoang Sa [Paracels] and Truong Sa [Spratlies]," and no participating country made any protest.[22]

Although claims and counterclaims to these islands continued, owing to the political circumstances existing in the 1950s and 1960s, the three major parties involved — Beijing, Taipei, and Saigon — never had an opportunity to confront one another at international conferences or settle their disputes through negotiations and could only make unilateral declarations.[23] Apparently, as a consequence, in 1968 the Philippines also advanced claims to the eastern part of the Spratlies (known to them as *Kalayaan* or Freedom Islands) thereby further complicating the legal status of this archipelago, though again, no occupation was attempted.[24] This situation persisted until February 1974 when China assumed full military control over all the Paracels, followed almost immediately by the occupation of six Spratly islands by Vietnam and five by the Philippines.[25] Because France was the first country to have occupied both island groups militarily, the dispute between China and Vietnam is essentially over whether discovery or prior occupation confers a stronger legal title. (See map 2.)

Map 2.   The South China Sea

Whereas the potential for conflict has clearly existed in all the three regions, no real territorial dispute occurred between Beijing and Hanoi throughout the 1950s and 1960s.[26] The reasons are not difficult to identify. First, Hanoi was engaged in a war with France and then with the United States and was dependent upon Chinese aid and support. For two full decades China was Vietnam's principal ally. After the bombing of North Vietnam in 1965, a good proportion of Vietnam's industrial and military facilities were moved from the Red River Delta to the mountainous areas along, if not across, the Sino-Vietnamese border; large numbers of civilian Vietnamese also frequently sought refuge in China; and a considerable amount of training and logistical activities took place inside Chinese territories.[27] It was the period when Mao Zedong proclaimed that "the 700 million Chinese people provide a powerful backing for the Vietnamese people; the vast expanse of China's territory is their reliable rear area."[28] The intensity of cross-border activities, particularly the constant flow of supplies, matériel, and personnel, made any delineation of boundaries both difficult and superfluous.

A similar situation existed in the Gulf of Tonkin, which constituted the main sea route for supply and communication between China and Vietnam, especially throughout the 1950s and during the early 1960s. According to the Chinese, there was friendly cooperation on such matters as shipping, fishery, and scientific research.[29] In the late 1950s, China reportedly even turned over to Vietnam some coastal islands in the Gulf inhabited for centuries by Chinese, apparently as a gesture of solidarity and generosity.[30] After the Tonkin incident of 1964, however, Hanoi lost control of much of the gulf to the U.S. Navy, and, consequently, there was no point in its making any claim to the sea area. As for the Paracels and the Spratlies, Hanoi could not have done less during this period. Apart from the geographical distance, both island groups lay off the South Vietnamese coast still under the jurisdiction of the hostile Saigon regime. Hanoi was simply in no position to challenge both Chinese claims and U.S. sea power at the same time. Thus, on June 15, 1956, Premier

Pham Van Dong reportedly said to China: "From the histori-cal point of view, these islands are Chinese territory."[31]

In September 1958, when China, in its declaration extend-ing the breadth of Chinese territorial waters to 12 nautical miles, specified that the decision applied to all Chinese ter-ritories, including the Paracels and the Spratlies, Hanoi again went on record to recognize China's sovereignty over the two archipelagoes. Pham Van Dong stated in a note to Chinese leader Zhou Enlai on September 14, 1958: "The Government of the Democratic Republic of Vietnam recognizes and sup-ports the declaration of the Government of the People's Re-public of China on its decision concerning China's territorial sea made on September 4, 1958."[32] As late as May 1965, when the United States designated the whole of Vietnam and the waters extending about 100 miles from the Vietnamese coast as the "combat zone" for U.S. armed forces, Hanoi condemned the action as having encroached upon "the territorial waters of the PRC in its Xisha Islands."[33]

The absence of any border dispute during this honey-moon, however, did not signify complete accord between China and Vietnam. The fact that North Vietnam was one of the only two Asian countries that did not conclude a bound-ary treaty with China in the late 1950s and early 1960s is evidence of possible reservations entertained by both sides. As recently revealed by Chinese and Vietnamese sources, there had always been a few sectors of the land boundary on which the two sides held different views.[34] As early as No-vember 1956, questions arose at local levels regarding the management of certain border areas lying between China's Guangdong and Guangxi Provinces and Vietnam's Hai Ninh, Lang Son, and Cao Bang Provinces.[35] Although the nature and scope of the dispute has never been disclosed, presuma-bly it resulted from the ambiguous delineation of adminis-trative responsibilities.

Consultation between local representatives of the two sides inevitably touched upon the boundary issue, which they could not resolve, and the matter was referred to central authorities for consideration.[36] In November 1957, the Secretariat of the Central Committee of the Vietnam Workers' Party (VWP) proposed, in a letter to the Secretariat of the Central Committee of the Chinese Communist Party (CCP), that both sides should maintain the status quo pending final settlement and that local authorities should be strictly forbidden to enter into negotiations or change the existing boundary line.[37] The fact that Hanoi took the initiative to shelve the issue temporarily may well indicate that it was not in a strong legal or political position to gain from any negotiation and preferred to wait for a more opportune time to settle the issue. In April 1958, the Central Committee of the CCP finally agreed to the Vietnamese request.[38]

On the South China Sea, signs of vacillation in Hanoi's position can also be detected regarding sovereignty over the Paracels and the Spratlies. Hanoi appeared willing to acquiesce to Chinese claims as long as Saigon remained more or less indifferent to the whole issue. But once Saigon made concrete efforts to assert its sovereignty over these islands, Hanoi became reluctant to take the opposite stand. This is so particularly after the late 1950s when tension began to build up between Beijing and Saigon over these archipelagoes.

In early 1959, a major confrontation occurred for the first time between China and South Vietnam over the Paracels, when Saigon, in an attempt to dislodge the Chinese, landed troops on one of the islands, kidnapped dozens of Chinese fishermen, and tore up the Chinese flag hoisted on the island. In March 1959, Saigon's naval gunboats again harassed Chinese fishermen on the Paracels. On both occasions, Beijing lodged strong protests against the South Vietnamese action, but throughout the course of the conflict Hanoi made no statement in support of the Chinese position.[39] Again, in 1961, when the Saigon government announced the incorporation of the Paracels into the Quang Nam Province over strong Chinese protests, Hanoi refrained from siding with China by keeping strict silence on the issue.[40]

In July 1973, Saigon began to issue oil exploration permits to foreign companies in areas near the Spratlies, and in September 1973, it went a step further by announcing the formal incorporation of 11 main islands in the Spratly group into Vietnam's Phuoc Tuy Province.[41] On both occasions, Hanoi once again failed to lend even verbal support to Beijing in spite of the strong Chinese protests reaffirming its "indisputable sovereignty" over all the four island groups in the South China Sea and the natural resources in the areas around them.[42] Similarly, no word of support was expressed by the Provincial Government of South Vietnam (the Viet Cong). The series of bold actions taken by Saigon in an attempt to reassert Vietnam's claims to these islands and the fact that they had met with only verbal protests from China clearly gave Hanoi second thoughts on the whole issue. The 1973 events, in particular, occurred after the Paris Cease-fire Agreement of that year, when the Soviet Union had begun to replace China as the principal supplier of arms to Vietnam. With the military situation in the south becoming increasingly volatile and with the Chinese role declining as the end of the Vietnam War approached, Hanoi apparently decided that a wait-and-see attitude was in its best interest.

2

Surfacing of the Conflict

The first signs of controversy between Beijing and Hanoi over territorial matters emerged in late December of 1973, when Vietnam informed China of its intention to prospect for oil in the Gulf of Tonkin and proposed negotiations to delineate the border in the Gulf officially.[43] That the Gulf of Tonkin was the first proposed topic of negotiation clearly signified its central importance to the entire territorial dispute. China agreed to negotiate but suggested that, while an agreement was being reached, all prospecting work should be kept out of a rectangular area formed by the eighteenth and twentieth parallels and the 107th and 108th meridians, an area of about 8,000 square miles that lies 40–80 miles off both countries and is about equidistant to their coastlines; China also proposed that no third country should be allowed in any exploration activity that might be undertaken.[44] Although at that time Hanoi had not yet specified how the gulf should be delineated, it clearly had in mind the water area beyond the 12-mile territorial waters and the hypothetical boundary drawn according to the principle of the median line – otherwise there would have been no urgent need either to inform or to negotiate with China. The Chinese apparently acted on the assumption that the red line specified in the Sino-French Convention of 1887 divided only the islands of the gulf, not its water area, otherwise Beijing would not have marked out as a neutral region the above-mentioned rectangular area, which lies to the west of the line. Because this was before the 200-mile economic zone had been sanctioned by international law, the Chinese presumably also wanted to avoid any future conflict between the two countries or with any third country before a bilateral agreement could be reached on the issue.

Before the Gulf of Tonkin issue could be settled, however, another territorial dispute exploded in late January 1974, when Chinese forces clashed with South Vietnamese troops over the Paracel Islands in a showdown for total control. In an official statement issued immediately after the defeat of the Saigon forces, Hanoi took the unprecedented stand that "the frequently complex disputes over territories and frontiers between neighbouring countries demand careful and circumspect examination. Countries involved should settle such disputes by negotiation and in a spirit of good-neighbourliness."[45] This position was also echoed by the Viet Cong.[46] This was also the first time that Hanoi had openly expressed disagreement with China over the territorial question. By recognizing the existence of disputes over these islands and, moreover, by pointing out their complex nature, Hanoi thus implicitly withdrew its previous recognition of Chinese claims to the islands. That the statement was issued after the effective occupation of the entire Paracel group by the Chinese further implied that Hanoi now entertained serious reservations about the Chinese action. Furthermore, Hanoi said nothing when Saigon seized six islands in the Spratly group in early February 1974 in retaliation against the Chinese occupation of the Paracels, thereby giving tacit support to Saigon's action.

The Paracels incident appeared to mark the turning point in Sino-Vietnamese relations as far as the territorial dispute is concerned. When negotiations on the division of the Gulf of Tonkin eventually took place in Beijing at the vice foreign minister's level in August 1974, North Vietnam took the position that the gulf had already been divided by the Sino-

French treaties and proposed to treat the whole of it as a "historical gulf" belonging only to China and Vietnam, with longitude 108°3'13" east – the red line specified in the 1887 Sino-French Convention – as the sea boundary between the two countries.[47]

The Chinese immediately rejected the idea on the grounds that the red line was no sea boundary line, for no reference whatsoever was made in the Convention to the gulf as such, and that neither China nor Vietnam had ever exercised sovereignty over or jurisdiction in the gulf area beyond their territorial seas.[48] In addition to the divergent interpretations of the Sino-French Conventions, the two sides also differed on where exactly the entrance of the gulf was supposed to lie.[49] Although no detailed information was released on this related issue, North Vietnam apparently wanted to mark the gulf apart from the water area of the South China Sea, whereas China was somewhat reluctant to do so.

That Hanoi should have brought up the hitherto least disputed issue for negotiation so early and insisted on the demarcation of the gulf and the division of its entire water area is interesting. Hanoi apparently had its eyes on the future settlement of the South China Sea islands and could well have been trying to preempt any Chinese attempt to apply the red line specified in the Sino-French boundary accords to all islands in the sea, as the Chinese government had done in the 1930s in its diplomatic correspondence with France. Indeed, unless Hanoi could get Beijing to agree that the red line was a sea boundary dividing only a historical gulf, which in turn was clearly separated from the South China Sea, it would be difficult for any Vietnamese government to claim legal title to the Paracels and the Spratlies, both of which lie to the east of the line.

Moreover, the whole idea of a historical gulf is significant. Because Vietnam and China are the only two countries that could make claims to the South China Sea islands by virtue of historical rights, if the Gulf of Tonkin could be set aside as a sea area shared by China and Vietnam exclusively on historical grounds, it would be difficult in the future for China to oppose a division of spheres of influence in the vast South China Sea on similar grounds. The Paracel Islands, which are closer to the Chinese island of Hainan and already occupied by China, could be marked as Chinese territory, and the remote Spratly group could be placed under Vietnamese jurisdiction. By the same token, if the concept of historical gulf was accepted by China, a historical borderline on land could also become irrefutable.

Whatever motives the Vietnamese might have had, the Chinese were apparently taken aback by the ambitious tone of the proposal, if not by its possible consequences. Although China did not necessarily intend to follow the arguments of its Kuomintang predecessors in refuting Vietnam – and had no way of doing so on a subject not yet on the agenda – the novelty of the North Vietnamese proposal could well have alerted China to the possible implications of the Vietnamese position and of Hanoi's territorial ambitions and therefore could not be concurred in lightly. To the extent that China refused to recognize the gulf as such in the treaties, its interpretation of the treaty provisions allowed China some room for maneuver on the South China Sea islands. In addition to its dubious tenability from the viewpoint of international law, the Vietnamese proposal was unacceptable to China for one practical reason: it would give nearly two-thirds of the gulf area to Vietnam and move the boundary close to Hainan. If China were to have less than a fair share of the gulf water, which is adjacent to the Chinese coast and in the immediate vicinity of Hainan, it would certainly be presumptuous for it to claim the Spratlies, which lie more than 600 miles off China's southernmost coast. Consequently the negotiations came to an abrupt end in November 1974 with no agreement reached.[50]

Subsequent events lend support to the foregoing speculation. In October 1974, when the Sino-Vietnamese negotiations were still in progress, Hoang Tung, a member of the Central Committee of the VWP and editor in chief of the party newspaper, *Guan Doi Nhan Dan*, in an interview with a Thai reporter went as far as to say: "China is not a country of this region and should not have as much offshore waters as it has claimed."[51] In April 1975, fewer than four months after the first round of negotiations broke down and before the fall of Saigon to the Communists, Hanoi dispatched troops to occupy the six islands in the Spratly group that had been seized by South Vietnam the year before.[52] Because of its failure to get Beijing to agree to the Vietnamese interpretation of the Sino-French boundary accords governing the Gulf of Tonkin, Hanoi apparently calculated that occupation of at least some of the Spratly Islands was the only way of backing up its claim to all the offshore islands and would at least give itself a strong bargaining hand vis-à-vis China, if not also create a fait accompli that China would have to recognize eventually. By the end of May, the entire Spratly group was marked as part of Vietnamese territory in a Vietnamese map carried by *Guan Doi Nhan Dan*.[53] Around the same time, Hanoi reportedly had also started to conduct talks with foreign oil companies on the resumption of oil exploration and exploitation in areas adjacent to this archipelago.[54] In late 1975, a new territorial map of the reunited Vietnam for the first time included the Paracels as well as the Spratlies.[55] It was quite clear by now that Vietnam was determined to challenge the Chinese claim of sovereignty over these islands.

China was clearly irritated, if not in fact dumbfounded, by all these unexpected moves on the part of Hanoi. But Beijing did not take any action until September 18, 1975, just before the visit of the Vietnamese Communist Party Secretary Le Duan to Beijing, when the *People's Daily* published six large photographs of the Paracels, apparently to remind the Vietnamese leader of the long-standing Chinese claim to these islands.[56] Although the territorial issue must have been brought up during the talks held between Le Duan and Chinese leaders, however, only a preliminary exchange of views was made, with no attempt to settle the issue, and no agreement was reached.[57] As if to persuade Vietnam to think twice, only one day after Le Duan left China, the *People's Daily* again published a picture of Chinese militia units stationed on the Paracels. On November 24, the *Guangming Daily* also carried a lengthy article presenting historical documents, archaeological evidence, and even foreign maps – including one published by the Soviet Union – to substantiate Chinese claims further.[58] In early 1976, a documentary film entitled "Islands of the South China Sea" was produced by the Chinese People's Liberation Army's August First Film Studio, which not only showed an early Chinese presence in all the four archipelagoes in the South China Sea but also depicted how a Chinese archaelogical team in the Paracels had uncovered ancient Chinese coins, porcelain, and other artifacts purportedly dating from the Tang (618–907 A.D.) and Sung (960–1297 A.D.) dynasties.[59]

Although Vietnam showed no intention of withdrawing from the six Spratly islands, it made no attempt to build up a strong case against China. In fact, throughout 1975–1976, Hanoi appeared to be adopting a relatively low-keyed approach to the issue. Whatever official references had been made to the Chinese sovereignty claims were often indirect and vague and were almost invariably confined to the Spratlies, over which it had more effective control.[60] In addition to the fact that the Paracels had already been occupied by China, presumably Vietnam might have found it difficult to claim sovereignty over this archipelago, even on legalistic grounds, before the issue of the Gulf of Tonkin was settled in its favor. Indeed, there was strong evidence that in 1976 Hanoi was prepared to strike a bargain with China on the basis of the more or less de facto situation in the South China Sea, that is, recognize Chinese sovereignty over the Paracels in exchange for Chinese recognition of Vietnamese sovereignty over the Spratlies. An official statement made by the Viet Cong on June 5, 1976 merely reaffirmed its "sovereignty with regard to the Truong Sa Islands," and reserved for itself "the right to protect that sovereignty," without mentioning the Paracels at all.[61]

An even clearer hint was dropped in July, almost immediately after the formal reunification of the two halves of Vietnam, when the editor in chief of *Guan Doi Nhan Dan* said openly to a Swedish journalist: "China should relinquish her sovereignty over the Spratlies, in return for the Vietnamese recognition of Chinese sovereignty over the Paracels."[62] Hanoi's intention became unmistakable by late July in Jakarta when Phan Hien, Vietnamese deputy foreign minister, officially commenting for the first time on the dispute over the South China Sea islands, declared that, whereas the Paracels and Spratlies were "now marked on the map as Vietnamese under the name of Hoang Sa and Truong Sa . . . a dispute about this territory must be settled by negotiation on the basis of *mutual understanding and equality*."[63] (Italics added.)

Nevertheless, whatever kind of political trade Hanoi might have been contemplating at that time, Beijing was firm on the issue of the South China Sea islands from the beginning and was not inclined to accept any compromise. To dispel any doubts about China's determination to safeguard its rights, the Chinese Foreign Ministry on June 14, 1976 issued the hitherto most strongly worded warning to Vietnam, without mentioning it by name:

> The Nansha Islands, as well as the Xisha, Zhongsa, and Dongsa islands, have always been part of the territory of China, which has indisputable sovereignty over them and the adjacent seas; any armed invasion and occupation, or exploration and exploitation of oil and other resources there by any foreign country constitute encroachements on China's territorial integrity and sovereignty and are impermissible.[64]

On August 31, apparently in reply to Hanoi's suggestion of sharing the South China Sea islands, China reiterated that Chinese claims to all the South China Sea islands were "fully proven" by historical evidence and archaeological finds and that these islands had been China's "sacred territory since ancient times and belong to the Chinese people."[65] Although neither China nor Vietnam had yet attacked each other directly, the territorial dispute was rapidly gathering heat, as protestations, thinly veiled threats, and counterthreats were made and repeated.

While the controversy over the Gulf of Tonkin and the offshore islands was heating up, a major dispute also surfaced over the land boundary. The approaching end of the Vietnam War, as signified by the Paris Cease-fire Agreement of January 1973, drew the attention of both China and Vietnam to the rather fluid situation along their 797-mile land border. The suspension of U.S. bombing of the north, in particular, led to a demand for better regulation of cross-border traffic and normalization of daily life, both of which necessitated a clearer delineation of administrative responsibilities in the border areas. Under these circumstances, controversies were revived in the disputed areas, and, in late 1974, Hanoi began to raise the issue of the "historical borderline" that had been allegedly violated by China.

Hanoi first charged that the joint points of the Hanoi-Youyiguan railway track at the Sino-Vietnamese border had been mistakenly placed by Chinese railway workers more than 300 meters inside Vietnamese territory in 1955.[66] Hanoi therefore proposed an adjustment of the track in accordance with the "historical borderline," which was flatly rejected by China on the grounds that the Chinese section of the railway line was entirely within Chinese territory according to the Sino-French boundary accords. In 1975, in the course of the joint laying of an oil pipeline across the border in the Van Lang district of Vietnam's Long Son Province, a similar dispute erupted as to where the junction of the pipeline was to be placed, and, because the two could not agree on the boundary that divides China and Vietnam, the entire project was suspended.[67]

Although these were among only a few cases that have been reported identically by both sides, between 1975 and 1977 Vietnam allegedly also made territorial claims on more than 15 places in Yunnan and Guangxi Provinces, and to sustain its claims, proceeded to remove or destroy some of the stone markers along the border, harass local Chinese residents, and divert the flow of certain boundary rivers.[68] In the meantime, Hanoi also charged China with destroying the "vestiges of the historical borderline" and encroaching upon Vietnamese territory by undertaking "massive projects of road building" in the border regions and by incorporating Vietnamese inhabitants into Chinese administrative units.[69] In all these cases, the "historical borderline" was a phrase repeatedly used by Vietnam, not the relevant Sino-French border Conventions. Presumably Hanoi was reclaiming those areas that China had helped administer during the war and, at the same time, reasserting its sovereignty over areas of Chinese territory that had long been under Vietnamese administration, though they might well lie beyond the boundary stipulated by the Sino-French Conventions.

In view of the small areas of contested territory and the trivial nature of the controversies raised over the land – particularly against the background of a 30-year-old close alliance – Hanoi might have deliberately played up its differences with China over the land boundary in order to show its displeasure over the gulf and South China Sea issues. It is no accident that the issue of the Hanoi-Youyiguan railway line was raised by Vietnam almost immediately after the negotiations on the Gulf of Tonkin broke down. If the status quo of the Paracels was not, from the Chinese point of view, a subject for negotiation, Vietnam could claim the status quo of the land border was a valid basis for realignment of the land boundary between the two countries. Nevertheless, precisely because the Vietnamese claims were made to tiny pieces of land, they caused much indignation among the Chinese, particularly among those residing along the border who had shared the hardships of the Vietnamese during the long war. From the Chinese point of view, the Vietnamese proposal to divide the Gulf of Tonkin was ambitious enough, but to make further claims to land territories was sheer greed and ingratitude that could not be tolerated.

As claims and counterclaims continued, confrontation between local authorities and residents of both sides inevitably led to acts of violence. Thus, in 1974 alone, more than 100 incidents reportedly took place along the border.[70] Whereas Vietnam appears to have taken the initiative at least in the beginning, if not in most of the cases, Beijing also admitted that some of these incidents had been caused by "violations of Chinese policies by Chinese local personnel."[71] These incidents clearly had a destabilizing effect on Sino-Vietnamese relations. Whether it was the border incidents that exacerbated the dispute over the offshore islands or vice versa, the heat generated by the controversies in the two areas of conflict was clearly accumulative.

As the gap between Chinese and Vietnamese positions widened over the offshore islands, tension also steadily built up along the land border, with the result that the number of incidents shot up to about 400 in 1975 and more than 900 in 1976.[72] In July 1976, apparently as a result of such border scuffles, the Chinese informed Vietnam of their intention to close the Chinese side of the Hanoi-Youyiguan railway for repairs, and Vietnam agreed. Yet when the repair work reached the 300-meter disputed section, hundreds of armed Vietnamese security men reportedly obstructed the repair work by destroying an already built railway embankment and by shoveling into a ditch tons of macadam and sand prepared by the Chinese workers. They also attacked the Chinese workers verbally through loudspeakers and with stones.[73] According to Vietnam, the Chinese took the opportunity to erect a number of structures on the disputed section in the same style as those on the Chinese section, thereby provoking "energetic protests" by the local people.[74] Whatever the validity of the charges and countercharges, it is probably also no coincidence that this first major incident erupted almost immediately after China's rejection of Vietnam's proposal to share the South China Sea islands and its strong warning to Vietnam about the islands.

Earlier, in March and September 1975, Beijing proposed to hold comprehensive negotiations on the territorial dispute, but Hanoi did not respond until June 1977, when Chinese Deputy Prime Minister Li Xiannian made a personal request in a meeting with visiting Vietnamese Premier Pham Van Dong.[75] The reasons for Hanoi's reluctance to negotiate in 1975 and 1976 are not difficult to understand. Detecting no sign of any modification in China's intransigence on the gulf and South China Sea issues and having no intention to make

any concessions itself, Hanoi apparently considered it point-
less to negotiate. At a time when the country was devastated
by a long war and the integration of the south with the north
had yet to be achieved, Hanoi also needed a breathing spell
and certainly lacked the power to bargain with China from
a position of strength.[76] To conduct comprehensive negotiations on territorial matters with Beijing after China's positions had become crystal clear meant that Vietnam either had
to concede to China's demands or confront China openly,
neither of which served Vietnam's interest at that time. Because the controversies over Kampuchea and the ethnic Chinese in Vietnam had not yet come into the open, Hanoi still
expected to receive substantial Chinese aid to assist in its
reconstruction projects. Thus Pham Van Dong sent a long
list of requested items to China as late as November 1976.[77]
Although the Soviet Union had already started to woo Vietnam enthusiastically, Hanoi was still trying to pursue a more-
or-less independent foreign policy and intended to keep all
options open, including normalization of relations with the
United States.[78]

By mid-1977, the situation was different. The expected
Chinese aid was not forthcoming. In February 1977, Beijing
formally notified Vietnam of China's inability to provide any
new aid, citing the interference and sabotage of the Gang of
Four and the disastrous Tang-shan earthquake, both occur-
ring in 1976 and presumably also distracting much of Beijing's attention from the border issue.[79] China's unwillingness
to help Vietnam, however, contrasted sharply with the escalating military and economic aid Beijing was rendering
Kampuchea's Pol Pot regime. In the meantime, Vietnam's
overtures to the United States repeatedly failed to strike a
responsive chord, while the Soviet Union was more eager
than ever to assist Vietnam both politically and financially.[80]
Because China's position on the territorial issues remained
firm, while its importance to Vietnam was declining rapidly,
the Soviet offer of a close relationship became irresistible.
Also, by mid-1977, Vietnam was formally reunified; the regime had more or less consolidated its grip upon the south;

and the nation was on the way to reconstruction and recovery. As a result of all these developments, Hanoi apparently decided that the time had come to deal with China from a position of strength.[81]

It is therefore no coincidence that in the course of 1977, the tension along the Sino-Vietnamese border mounted rapidly, and Hanoi's positions on all the territorial issues under dispute also steadily hardened. In April 1977, the Chinese government again proposed to carry out urgent repair work on the disputed section of the Hanoi-Youyiguan railway, and Vietnam again agreed. But on May 4, 1977, no sooner had the work started than the first bloody border incident erupted: more than 500 Vietnamese troops reportedly moved into the area and wounded 51 Chinese workers, 6 of them seriously.[82]

Only a week later, on May 12, the Foreign Ministry of Vietnam, disregarding China's position, proceeded to define Vietnam's territorial waters, continental shelf, and exclusive economic zone and to apply them to "all the islands and archipelagoes belonging to Vietnamese territory and situated outside the territorial waters" of Vietnamese coast, which could only mean the Paracels and the Spratlies. The same statement also specifically stipulated that Vietnam's economic zone extended 200 miles from its coast, which included the greater portion of the Gulf of Tonkin and cut into the two archipelagoes in the South China Sea.[83] In June 1977, when Chinese Vice Premier Li Xiannian reminded Pham Van Dong that Hanoi had made statements in support of Chinese sovereignty over the Spratlies and the Paracels in the past and should not have changed its stand after 1974, Dong reportedly replied that it had been "a matter of necessity" to recognize Chinese sovereignty over these islands during the Vietnam War, because Vietnam had had to "place resistance to the U.S. imperialism above everything else."[84] Dong now insisted that the Vietnamese note addressed to China in September 1958 referred only to the 12-mile territorial waters and had to be understood "in the context of the historical circumstances of the time."[85] Clearly Hanoi was now determined to face China squarely on the territorial dispute.

3

Futile Negotiations

When the second round of negotiations on the boundary
question finally started in Beijing in October 1977 at the vice
foreign minister's level, the gap between the Chinese and
Vietnamese positions was already too wide to be bridged.
Although China apparently had sought to discuss all three
areas of conflict, the new round of talks dealt only with the
land boundary and Gulf of Tonkin issues, not with the South
China Sea islands.[86] Presumably this was in part because of
the more urgent nature of border clashes and their more immediate impact upon Sino-Vietnamese relations and in part
because the land boundary and the Gulf of Tonkin, being
strictly a bilateral matter between China and Vietnam and
regulated explicitly by the Sino-French treaties, would be
easier to settle than the issue of the South China Sea islands.
Having become aware of each other's positions on the South
China Sea islands, it was also quite clear that a solution to
the land boundary and the Gulf of Tonkin had to come before
the more thorny and politically sensitive dispute over the
vast South China Sea could be solved.[87]

Nevertheless, no sooner had the talks started than a fundamental difference emerged between the two parties in their
overall perception of the two issues and in their order of
priorities. Hanoi's basic position was that the boundary be-

tween China and Vietnam both on land and in the Gulf of Tonkin had already been clearly delineated by the 1887 and 1895 Sino-French boundary conventions, and, except for a few disputed areas, the treaties should be strictly respected.[88] Specifically in reference to the Gulf of Tonkin, Hanoi reiterated its previous position: according to the French text, the Sino-French boundary accords had delimited not only the islands but also the waters of the gulf, and, therefore, Vietnam was entitled to the entire sea area west of the red line specified in the accords.[89]

With respect to the land boundary, Hanoi contended that in the 1957–1958 exchanges of letters between the Communist parties of the two countries, both sides had already confirmed the borderline and had agreed to maintain the status quo.[90] Hanoi asserted that the two sides needed only to reaffirm their intention to respect the existing boundary and that this was the most basic principle on which all boundary issues could be settled.[91] Hanoi even proposed a draft agreement containing this principle for immediate signature as a preliminary step toward settling whatever minor disputes might exist between the two countries. Moreover, Hanoi insisted that the land boundary and the sea boundary must be treated as one whole question, and the Gulf of Tonkin issue, in particular, should be settled first because the treaty terms were clear.[92]

The Chinese immediately challenged Hanoi's position. Beijing contended that, whereas the provisions of the Sino-French accords were generally clear, they should serve only as a basis for a negotiated settlement, precisely because of the existence of disputes and the discrepancies between treaty terms and the actual borderline.[93] The Chinese therefore proposed a thorough, joint rechecking of the alignment of the entire boundary against the accords, with a view to concluding a new treaty to replace the old ones.[94] For China, the 1958 agreement between Beijing and Hanoi to maintain the status quo along the land boundary was only a modus vivendi, and it by no means implied that a final delineation of disputed areas was to follow the line of actual jurisdiction.[95] With

regard to the Gulf of Tonkin, Beijing once again flatly rejected the Vietnamese interpretation of the boundary accords
as "fantastic" and "absurd from the viewpoint of international
law" and was prepared to discuss only a demarcation of economic zones on "a fair and reasonable basis."[96] Apart from
the Chinese text of the Sino-French boundary accords, which
Beijing cited to support its views, China's arguments were
essentially the same as those made in 1974, namely that
neither China nor Vietnam had ever exercised sovereignty
over or jurisdiction in the gulf beyond their territorial seas
and that no country had ever recognized it as a historical gulf.
In fact, China refused to consider the two territorial issues
as linked in any way and insisted that the land boundary be
the first item for discussion because it was more substantive
and immediately relevant.[97]

The divergent stands taken by the two reflected their different stakes in the dispute, which were not necessarily visible on the surface. Hanoi, which had benefited from the historical developments of recent decades, clearly wanted to
preserve the status quo of the land border and therefore the
total validity of relevant treaties with all their technical ambiguities. To agree to recheck the alignment of the entire land
boundary against the treaty provisions was to open a Pan-
dora's box, from which Vietnam would have little to gain but
much to lose. Generally satisfied with the actual land boundary but not yet on an equal footing with China in the South
China Sea, Hanoi naturally focused its attention on the Gulf
of Tonkin as the more important issue. Because both the land
boundary and the Gulf of Tonkin were governed by the treaties, Hanoi wanted to treat them as a single question. Such
an approach would also have the advantage of solving both
problems once a breakthrough was achieved on either of
them. Beijing, on the other hand, sought to recover territories
that had been lost to Vietnam over the past century or so
and insisted on the need to realign the land boundary according to the treaties and remove whatever ambiguities might
exist. Already in control of the Paracels and generally satisfied with the status quo in the Gulf of Tonkin, Beijing con-

sidered the land border the only substantive issue still to be settled. By insisting on treating each issue separately, China not only could strengthen its bargaining hand with respect to the land border but could also avoid any potential pitfalls.

Even when the two sides finally agreed to shelve the gulf issue temporarily, the conflict over the land did not become more amenable to solution, although the nature of the conflict became clearer with further exposition of views by both sides. Although both Vietnam and China enlisted the Sino-French boundary accords as a source of support, neither side was entirely consistent in its interpretation of these accords. Generally speaking, however, the Chinese position appeared to be relatively clearer: China insisted that the accords should be followed strictly with respect to the land boundary and that areas under the jurisdiction of one side that lay beyond the boundary line specified in the accords should, in principle, be returned to the other side unconditionally, although readjustments on an agreed, fair and reasonable basis might be made in a small number of cases.[98]

With regard to boundary rivers, which make up nearly one-third of the entire length of the land frontier, however, China took the position that the Sino-French treaties were not always clear with their references to the "median line." Beijing thus proposed to divide boundary rivers in accordance with existing international law and as explicitly mentioned in at least two of the boundary conventions: the boundary should follow the central line of the main channel in the case of navigable rivers and the thalweg of the main channel in the case of unnavigable rivers, and the ownership of the islands and sandbars in these rivers should be determined accordingly.[99] On the basis of these two principles, China proposed a joint survey of the entire boundary to delimit the alignment, and, after a thorough check, a new Sino-Vietnamese boundary treaty should be concluded to replace the old accords and new boundary markers erected to delimit the boundary.[100]

The Vietnamese position was diametrically opposed to the Chinese. On the issue of boundary rivers, Vietnam con-

tended that the Chinese principle of dividing rivers and islands applied only where it was specifically stated, that is,
to a small number of specified boundary rivers, according to
the Sino-French boundary conventions, and therefore should
not be adopted as a valid general principle.[101] In other words,
all water courses that had not been so demarcated should be
divided strictly according to their median lines as vaguely
specified in the boundary accords, irrespective of where the
main channel or thalweg might lie. As in the case of the Gulf
of Tonkin, Vietnam insisted on following the exact wording
of the treaty terms. In view of the topography of the Sino-
Vietnamese frontier, with mountain slopes higher to the north
than to the south and with most of the rivers running from
west to east, presumably such a rule would give more advantage to Vietnam than to China, because the main channels
of most, if not all, rivers tend to be closer to the southern
bank than to the northern one.

With regard to other land territories, however, Vietnam
took the ambiguous stand that whereas the Sino-French conventions should be observed, the "status quo of the borderline
left by history" should also be maintained.[102] Because this is
a phrase that was repeatedly used by Vietnam during the
talks, it could only mean that areas that had been historically
under Vietnamese jurisdiction should also be considered Vietnamese. Thus, Hanoi objected to the "unconditional" return
of all territories administered by either side beyond the borderline and insisted that attention should be given to the interests of local populations who had settled through "a long
process of history."[103] This implied that there were more
Chinese territories under de facto Vietnamese jurisdiction
than Vietnamese territories under Chinese administration.
For Hanoi, there was no need to recheck the entire boundary,
and the Chinese proposal to realign it was only a sinister
design to "alter the historical boundary line."[104]

Whereas the scope of dispute over the land boundary appeared to be rather small, the implications of the other territorial issues were something neither side could afford to
overlook. For the Chinese, an unquestioning acceptance of

the Vietnamese view that the Sino-French boundary was already clearly demarcated would immediately nullify all Chinese claims to the contested land areas. To concur in Hanoi's rigid interpretation of the treaty terms regarding boundary rivers would also imply China's acquiescence to Hanoi's interpretation of the Gulf of Tonkin issue. But that was not all. To agree with Vietnam on the Gulf of Tonkin would not only mean a loss of at least 5,000 square miles of waters, but also might well call into question Chinese claims to the Spratlies, which were more than 600 miles off China's southernmost coast. To concede to the "historical borderline" on land could also make it difficult for China to oppose a similar "historical borderline" in the Gulf of Tonkin and even-tually another "historical borderline" in the South China Sea. Only by insisting on the need for rechecking the actual land boundary against the treaty provisions could China hope to regain control over territories that had fallen under Viet-namese administration. Only by sticking to the prevailing rules of international law governing boundary rivers could China expect to gain a fair share of the waters in the Gulf of Tonkin. Indeed, to accept the principle of status quo on land after the Spratlies had been forcibly seized by Vietnam would simply be an act of timidity, which Beijing could not commit without implying Chinese ambivalence toward the legal status of this archipelago. Without being able even to discuss the offshore islands issue during the talks, China ap-parently calculated that only when Vietnam could be brought to agree in principle to the negotiability of the land issue could China hope to regain full sovereignty over all the South China Sea islands without further use of force. So the three issues of dispute were actually interwoven.

If China did not want to lose more, Vietnam was also determined to hold on to its gains. From Hanoi's point of view, to concede to the Chinese on the Gulf of Tonkin would seriously weaken Hanoi's claims to the Paracels and the Spratlies. Until Beijing showed its willingness to share the South China Sea islands with Vietnam by recognizing Viet-nam's sovereignty over the Spratlies, Hanoi had to insist that the Gulf of Tonkin was already divided. This is because Hanoi could never be sure that China would not once again interpret the treaty terms governing the gulf in a broad sense so as to include islands in the South China Sea, particularly in view of the fact that China had not recognized any specific reference to the gulf in the relevant treaties. Until China could be brought to accept the Vietnamese interpretation of the treaty terms concerning the Gulf of Tonkin, there was no point in Vietnam's giving up any of the contested land areas, which after all had been mostly under Vietnamese control. To allow flexibility on the boundary rivers or to adopt the thalweg principle for such rivers would make the Vietnamese position on the Gulf of Tonkin untenable. To retreat from the land border would also imply a retreat from the principle of the status quo, from which Hanoi could only benefit. Because the Sino-French boundary accords were the most authoritative legal documents regulating the territorial issues between China and Vietnam, only when Hanoi insisted that the accords were clear both on land and sea issues and were therefore more or less nonnegotiable, could Hanoi keep what it already had and yet still make new demands on China. After all, Hanoi was clearly aware of China's inability to take over the Spratly islands by force in the foreseeable future. Therefore, its continuing occupation of the six Spratly islands could only benefit Vietnam in the long run.

Although both China and Vietnam had focused their attention on the South China Sea, their positions had even broader implications. From the Chinese point of view, all the so-called unequal treaties signed by the Imperial Chinese government with foreign countries in the nineteenth century should be in principle negotiable, if only because of their dubious legal quality, their technical ambiguities, and the fact that they were politically outmoded. This has been China's consistent stand on all territorial disputes with its neighbors and in the conclusion of new treaties. Although Beijing may not have had Kampuchea in mind yet, to accept the complete validity of the Sino-French boundary accords would immediately call into question China's claims to territories involved in other disputes, such as with India and the Soviet Union. To agree to the principle of status quo or the historical legacy of colonialism, moreover, would certainly invalidate China's claims to other Chinese territories still under the occupation of foreign countries or hostile regimes, such as Hong Kong, Macao, and Taiwan, which was clearly unacceptable to Beijing.

From the Vietnamese point of view, the Sino-French treaties were virtually sacrosanct as they had led not only to the separation of Vietnam from China and Vietnamese independence but also to the establishment of a union of Indochinese states, which Hanoi – as subsequent events showed – had every intention of reviving. With at least 20 thousand troops still entrenched on Kampuchean soil and already in a process of exercising effective control over Laos, Hanoi's stress upon the status quo and the legacy of history was in fact necessary for it to hold on to the large strips of territory in Kampuchea and to justify its dominant position in Laos. Therefore, in clinging firmly to the concept of historical legacy at home, Hanoi in fact was also looking beyond its land borders to the west. Only by insisting on the sanctity of the Sino-French boundary conventions, could Hanoi acquire legitimacy in building its own regional empire.

As the differences between China and Vietnam over territorial issues involved matters of principle with far-reaching implications, the gap between the two sides was actually wider than it appeared, and neither could afford to give in lightly, particularly at a time of changing alliance patterns in Southeast Asia. No wonder the negotiations dragged on for more than 10 months and, in all that time, the two sides failed even to reach agreement on the procedure for conducting the talks on the boundary question. The talks were suspended in June 1978.[105]

4

The Road to War

Because of its broad implications, the drawn-out territorial dispute not only generated much ill will on both sides but also alerted each country to the other's overall intentions in Indochina. The dispute became quickly intertwined with, if it did not actually contribute to, the surfacing of two other issues of conflict – the ethnic Chinese in Vietnam and the war in Kampuchea – that were soon to engulf both nations and further exacerbate the territorial dispute. The recurrent incidents along the land border, which apparently reflected a growing restlessness among the border residents, inevitably raised the question of their loyalty. Yet because there were more Chinese territories and residents under Vietnamese administration, the problem facing the local Vietnamese authorities was much more serious as it tended to weaken Vietnamese claims to the contested areas. In fact, there is evidence that, because of China's stature and its role as benefactor throughout the Vietnam War, as well as the better economic conditions on the Chinese side of the border, many minority groups in the border regions had preferred to be placed under Chinese rather than Vietnamese rule, and Hanoi had to conduct education and propaganda activities among such groups to attract them to Vietnam.[106]

As unrest spread along the land border, the situation became more and more untenable for Hanoi. In April of 1977, Hanoi launched a "purification" campaign along the Chinese border, which involved the ejection of overtly or potentially disloyal Chinese residents and pro-Chinese minority groups from all the disputed areas.[107] Hanoi presumably calculated that once all the non-Vietnamese residents were removed, the dispute over territorial sovereignty would die down. By October 1977, when the Sino-Vietnamese talks on territorial matters were under way, this border purification process was at its height, and the Chinese residents and non-Vietnamese minority groups who had long been settled in the border areas either left because of fear or were forced across into Chinese territory.[108] Although the numbers affected were relatively small, Beijing could not overlook the implications for the large and economically powerful Chinese community in Vietnam. Viewed together with other measures taken against the ethnic Chinese in the course of 1977, the move clearly foreshadowed a major crisis.[109]

The territorial dispute also hastened a basic policy reorientation by Vietnam with respect to Kampuchea and a concomitant renewal of the alliance between Beijing and Phnom Penh. To Vietnam, China's insistence on an exclusive right to all the South China Sea islands and particularly its refusal to accept the legacy of French colonialism, clearly implied that Beijing was not about to acquiesce to a dominant Vietnamese position in either Kampuchea or Laos. China's adamant stance on all the issues of territorial dispute at a time of the worsening border dispute between Vietnam and Kampuchea seemed to be a deliberate effort to slight Vietnam vis-à-vis Kampuchea and to obstruct Hanoi's drive toward reasserting its status as a major regional power. To China, Hanoi's about-face with regard to territorial issues even before the Vietnam War ended in 1975 was already a clear enough sign of Vietnam's ingratitude. China feared it had an arrogant and ambitious neighbor whose conduct must be restrained. Indeed, from Beijing's perspective Vietnam's simultaneous

border disputes with China and Kampuchea, and particularly
the similarity of Vietnam's positions on the two disputes,
revealed Hanoi's expansionist designs in the region.[110]

In light of the above, it was necessary for Vietnam to
adopt a more militant and aggressive policy toward Kampuchea and, at least as a security measure, to put pressure
on all the ethnic Chinese in Vietnam. Such actions would
demonstrate not only Vietnamese displeasure but also its
ability to exert pressure on China and to attain its goals in
Kampuchea. Presumably a fait accompli in Kampuchea
would also strengthen Vietnam's claims to, and bargaining
power in, the disputed territories in the north and to the east.
On the other hand, as China came to view its territorial
dispute with Vietnam as a reflection of Hanoi's territorial ambitions in Indochina and a product of its deliberately anti-
China stance, Beijing also felt increasingly obligated to tilt
toward Kampuchea in the rapidly deepening Vietnam-Kampuchea conflict and to declare its support for the ethnic Chinese in Vietnam. Apart from showing disapproval of and protest over Vietnam's China and ethnic Chinese policies and
curbing Vietnam's regional ambitions, a firm stand on the
ethnic Chinese and Kampuchean issues and additional pressures applied to Vietnam would also enhance the chance of
safeguarding China's interests in the disputed territories.

It was therefore no coincidence that a quick succession
of events unfolded in late 1977 and early 1978 that led to a
rapid deterioration of Sino-Vietnamese relations: A sudden
outbreak of large-scale fighting along the Kampuchean-Vietnamese border in the last months of 1977 was soon followed
by an overt display of Chinese support for Phnom Penh in
January 1978.[111] A further escalation of the anti-Chinese campaign in Vietnam toward the end of 1977, which culminated
in a nationwide clampdown on Chinese bourgeois elements
in March 1978, was also accompanied by China's repeated
affirmation of its close links with overseas Chinese and its
pledge to protect their legitimate interests.[112]

Whatever the actual linkage among the three different
areas of conflict, the emergence of new issues of controversy

between China and Vietnam apparently further poisoned their relations and exacerbated the territorial dispute. The escalating war between Vietnam and Kampuchea only confirmed China's suspicions of Vietnamese ambitions, while the accelerated persecution of Chinese in Vietnam showed the ruthlessness with which Hanoi pursued its goals. For the Vietnamese, China's open support for Kampuchea and for the ethnic Chinese exposed China's opposition to a stable and powerful Vietnam and the degree to which Beijing was willing to sabotage Vietnam's drive toward independence and prestige. As a result, the two sides became more entrenched in their positions on the territorial dispute, for to do otherwise would imply a retreat from the escalating confrontation and a surrender in the other two issues of conflict.

The most immediate impact of their rapidly worsening relations was on the stability of the land border. As a result of deliberate encouragement by Hanoi and sheer panic among the Chinese communities in Vietnam, during the four months of March through June 1978, more than 100 thousand Chinese nationals crossed into China by land.[113] By July, the exodus had become a major international crisis when the number of Chinese fleeing or expelled to China exceeded 150 thousand. This massive influx not only created an intolerable financial burden on local Chinese authorities but also seriously complicated the security problems along the entire border. For months the Chinese authorities were at a loss as to how to cope with the situation. On July 11, 1978, when there seemed to be no end to the exodus, Beijing finally decided to close the entire border to stop the human flow.[114] This measure turned out to be far from effective, however, as Vietnam was determined to continue the exodus.

The controversy over the refugees inevitably added new fuel to the territorial dispute by multiplying problems of jurisdiction and creating new areas of contest as both sides attempted to secure new vantage positions in increasingly tense encounters. To preempt or retaliate against hostile acts, both countries could not have avoided venturing from time to time into places that were claimed by the other. As a result, clashes between border guards became unavoidable and incidents of violence began to be reported in May. The hitherto most serious incident, which resulted in the killing of four Chinese and wounding of dozens, took place on August 25 at Youyinguan where the disputed 300-meter-long railway is located.[115] This was followed almost immediately by the occupation of the Bonien Ridge on the Chinese side of the border checkpoint by 200 armed Vietnamese on August 28 and the blocking of the Friendship Bridge of the Sino-Vietnamese railway line by Hanoi on August 30.[116]

Once armed incidents had broken out, they inevitably generated more violent incidents and brought more troops to both sides of the border. By September 1978, China had already accused Vietnam of sending large numbers of armed personnel across the border to seize farmland, harass the peasants, dig trenches, erect barracades, lay mines, and even kidnap and fire at Chinese border guards and residents.[117] In turn, Vietnam charged China with repeated intrusions to carry out provocations, assaults, sabotage, and "nibbling activities," and, in particular, to "grab Vietnamese land which China claimed to be Chinese."[118] According to Beijing, from August 25 to December 15, 1978, Vietnam sent a total of 2,000 armed personnel to invade more than 100 areas of China's Guangxi region, instigating 200 border incidents — 100 in the Youyiguan area alone. As a result, Hanoi had "nibbled away large tracts of Chinese territory" and caused the death of "several dozens" of Chinese residents.[119] According to Hanoi, during the same period China provoked 137 border incidents and intruded into 38 Vietnamese areas with a total of 2,134 troops.[120] The situation appeared to be getting rapidly out of control. It certainly made normal traffic between the two countries all but impossible. Thus, on December 22, China decided to suspend all international train services at the Sino-Vietnamese border.[121]

Although both China and Vietnam must be held responsible for the steady escalation of tension along the land border, judging from the nature and pattern of the border incidents, and with the benefit of hindsight, the initiative appeared to be in the Vietnamese hands until mid-December of 1978. China appeared both unable and unwilling to react forcibly to the rapid unfolding of events, if only because of the large and steadily growing numbers of refugees on the Chinese side of the land border. Although increasingly alarmed by Vietnam's Chinese policy and its regional ambitions, until December 1978 Beijing was still unsure of the extent to which Hanoi would go to oppose China and to attain Vietnam's goals in Kampuchea.[122] After all, unable to provide effective help to either the Kampucheans or the Chinese in Vietnam, Beijing had apparently realized by the late summer of 1978 the limitations of its power and could not have deliberately escalated the scale of the border conflict with Vietnam.[123] It is thus perhaps no accident that, whereas Beijing reported Vietnamese armed encroachments upon China to have started in late August of 1978 and become most serious in the last two months of the year, Vietnamese sources reported that Chinese encroachments did not take place until late October of 1978 and were not serious until February 1979.[124] In addition to taking the lead in making accusations of territorial encroachments throughout 1978, China's charges were also invariably specific, often complete with names of places and persons affected, whereas Vietnam's charges were almost always general and vague, as well as less frequent, until the end of the year.[125] As late as early December 1979, China exercised considerable restraint in its order to the border security forces that "absolutely banned" the use of weapons in dealing with Vietnamese armed incursions.[126]

Vietnam was clearly in a more advantageous position in its expanding conflict with China. Having cleared the border of civilians, Hanoi was logistically freer to challenge Chinese power. With plans for a military campaign against Kampuchea made final in the last quarter of 1978, Vietnam needed to dramatize its conflict with China and to heighten the tension along their border, if only to enlist as much Soviet support as possible. After Vietnam began to implement its plans for the Kampuchean operation in November, a bold posture by the Vietnamese along the Sino-Vietnamese border presumably would dissuade China from possible intervention. No wonder that the day before the Soviet-Vietnamese Treaty of Friendship and Cooperation was signed, Hanoi reported the hitherto biggest armed clash between Chinese and Vietnamese troops that led to the death of six Chinese and "many Vietnamese."[127] Vietnam's growing confidence in dealing with China was further shown in the continuing massive exodus of Chinese across the land border in the last months of 1978, in spite of the stringent control measures adopted by China after mid-July.[128] By the end of 1978, a total of 200 thousand ethnic Chinese had been expelled by land.[129]

But that was not all. By mid-December, Vietnam reportedly had seized a number of strategic hills hundreds of meters inside Chinese territory and had begun shelling Chinese villages with mortar fire.[130] This was immediately followed by the Vietnamese Navy's firing upon Chinese fishing boats and killing Chinese fishermen in the Gulf of Tonkin.[131] On December 26, Hanoi sent a message to China reasserting sovereignty over the 300-meter track of the Sino-Vietnamese railway line from the point of junction to the border line.[132] On December 30, 1978, Hanoi issued its boldest statement on the two island groups in the South China Sea. Apart from declaring both archipelagoes "indisputable" Vietnamese territories and pledging Vietnam's determination to defend them, the statement warned – in much the same tone and with almost the same words as the statement made by Beijing in June 1976 – that "any foreign exploration, survey, exploitation, or occupation of the Truong Sa and Hoang Sa archipelagoes and of the contiguous areas . . . is illegal."[133] In January 1979, almost immediately after Vietnam seized Phnom Penh, Hanoi even declared that the Chinese occupation of the Paracels in 1974 was "no more justified than the occupation of the eastern group of this archipelago some twenty years before," thereby laying claim also to the tiny Pratas 200 miles northeast of the Paracels.[134] Apparently convinced of China's inability to respond effectively to its challenge along the land border, Hanoi seemed determined to present the maximum demands on territorial matters, if only to put itself on an equal footing with Beijing. Between September 1978 and February 1979, more than 700 armed provocations were reportedly instigated by Vietnam, resulting in the death of more than 300 Chinese frontier guards and inhabitants.[135]

Vietnam's increasingly hostile actions exposed the inadequacy of China's response and the dangerous implications of its continuing inaction. Without being able to negotiate further with Vietnam, with its security controls along the border seriously jeopardized by the continuing, unabated influx of refugees, and with no prospect of bringing peace and tranquility to the border areas, China had few alternatives but to resort to the use of force. As the number of violent incidents both on land and at sea continued to grow, what had hitherto been a relatively minor worry that Vietnam might launch armed attacks on other disputed territories was being turned into a real fear. After 200 thousand Chinese had been driven across the border and several hundreds of Chinese civilians and border guards killed, China's failure to act with determination in face of new Vietnamese claims and threats to Chinese territory would constitute an unmistakable admission of China's timidity and impotence. Not only would it encourage Vietnam to expel more Chinese overland, but it might also invite Hanoi to embark upon further territorial adventures against China particularly against the Paracels and the Spratlies, which China had no way of defending.

These considerations, in addition to other broader political factors, prompted China to harden its posture toward the end of 1978 and pushed it steadily to the edge of war. China's inclination to use force against Vietnam on a large scale became increasingly clear during December when Beijing, in response to a new spate of border incidents, issued a series of protests to Hanoi in which it repeatedly warned Vietnam not to "take China's restraint for a sign of weakness" or to "turn a deaf ear" to China's warnings.[136] Such admonitions peaked on December 24, when Beijing sent two successive notes of protests in one day to Vietnam immediately following another round of Vietnamese incursions that resulted in nine Chinese killed or wounded. While citing in detail the

most recent incidents of Vietnamese provocations in one of
the notes, Beijing went to great lengths in the other to enu-
merate how the Vietnamese after 1974 and "particularly since
the reunification of Vietnam" had made false claims to the
South China Sea, how they had first proposed to delimit the
Gulf of Tonkin and then gone back on their own words by
declaring that the Gulf was already demarcated, and how
they had stirred up the disputes along the erstwhile friendly
land border by harassing Chinese villages, kidnapping Chinese, and engineering violent incidents.[137]

In view of Vietnam's "insatiable, expansionist territorial
designs," China went on to deliver the hitherto most strongly
worded warning to Vietnam when it declared

> Vietnam has gone far enough in pursuing her anti-China
> course. There is a limit to the Chinese people's forbear-
> ance and restraint. China has never bullied and will
> never bully any other country; neither will it allow itself
> to be bullied by others. It will never attack unless it is
> attacked. But if it is attacked, it will certainly counterat-
> tack. China means what it says. We wish to warn the
> Vietnamese authorities that if they, emboldened by Mos-
> cow's support, try to seek a foot after gaining an inch
> and continue to act in this unbridled fashion, they will
> decidedly meet with the punishment they deserve. We
> state this here and now. Do not complain later that
> we've not given you a clear warning in advance.[138]

While the unusual phraseology of the statement already
hinted at China's changing disposition, subsequent warnings
made by China became even more blunt in language and bit-
ter in tone. In early January 1979, China began to speak of
"teaching Vietnam a lesson," and the phrase was repeated in
late January by Vice Premier Deng Xiaoping and again in
early February.[139]

Beijing's readiness to embark upon a major military
operation against Vietnam was evident in the sudden, rapid
buildup of armed forces on the border in late December 1978
and early January 1979. By February, China had assembled

330,000 ground troops, 1,200 tanks, at least 1,500 pieces of heavy artillery, and nearly 1,000 combat aircraft along the Sino-Vietnamese land border, and an unusually large Chinese fleet also gathered off Hainan Island.[140] By late December, Beijing admitted openly that the Chinese militia had been "driven beyond the limits of forbearance" and was therefore "compelled to fight back in self-defense" against the Vietnamese intruders.[141] From then on China no longer hesitated to initiate counterattacks and exploratory raids into Vietnamese territory, as revealed by the steady escalation in Hanoi's accusations about Chinese armed incursions into Vietnam in January 1979 as compared with the corresponding toning down of similar Chinese accusations during the same period. Vietnam claimed 230 Chinese intrusions in the first 40 days of 1979 compared to 583 for all of 1978, whereas China claimed 1,108 Vietnamese attacks for 1978 and only 129 in 1979 up until the Chinese invasion on February 17.[142]

By January 1979, the series of armed attacks and counterattacks had generated its own momentum and the increasingly bloody and chaotic land border could no longer be pacified without resort to more force. Although Beijing's decision to invade Vietnam was apparently made with other political objectives in view, had China's vital interests and territorial integrity not been directly threatened, Beijing clearly would have chosen its options more cautiously and would have found it difficult to justify a large-scale military action against Vietnam, particularly in view of the high risk of confrontation with the Soviet Union.[143] Viewed in this light, the territorial dispute was a major contributing factor to the Sino-Vietnamese border war in February 1979.

In launching the invasion into Vietnam on February 17, 1979, China called it a "counter-attack in self-defense" that had been forced upon it and identified the immediate cause of the military operation as Vietnam's "wanton" and "incessant" armed provocations and territorial encroachments, which had led to "a rapid deterioration" of the border situation and also "gravely threatened the peace and security of China's southern borders." Beijing further declared that the purpose of the operation was no more than "to ensure a peaceful and stable frontier" and to show that "China would never allow any other country to tamper with her territory" in such an unbridled manner.[144] In marching into Vietnam, Chinese troops stretched the battlefront across almost the entire border by launching attacks simultaneously in as many as 26 places.

The war showed China's determination to cripple at any cost the Vietnamese military establishment that had been built along the disputed border.

To drive home the lesson Beijing intended to administer to Vietnam, China made the capture of Lang Son, the strategic outpost guarding the gateway to the heart of the Red River Delta, the climax of China's military operations. The fall of Lang Son, which occurred on March 4, carried a particular symbolic meaning for the Chinese not only because Lang Son is the city nearest to Youyiguan — the center of the border dispute — but also because, historically, it was the last bulwark against Chinese military penetration in virtually all Sino-Vietnamese wars. Moreover, to leave the Vietnamese with few facilities on the border to resume territorial encroachments and armed harassments, Chinese troops undertook to destroy the entire communication infrastructure, including bridges, rail, roads, factories, and power plants, as well as all military installations.[145]

Although the Chinese invasion involved as many as 100 thousand troops and produced some of the fiercest ground battles in the history of Indochina wars, it was an operation executed within strictly defined limits meant to be no more than a lesson. Although commonly referred to as a month-long war, the major fighting actually lasted for only 17 days — from February 17 to March 5. In spite of the concentration of a large number of Chinese combat aircraft on the Chinese side of the border and an impressive show of Chinese naval strength off the Vietnamese coast, Beijing held back its air and naval forces throughout the hostilities. Despite Hanoi's exaggerations of the objectives of the Chinese invasion, the military operation targeted the two dozen or so cities and towns along the border, and, except in the remote Lai Chau Province, Chinese troops never advanced more than 25 miles into Vietnam, nor did they attempt to establish permanent control over those disputed areas that China had considered part of its territories or seize Vietnamese territory for bargaining purposes.[146] On the contrary, unlike any nation engaged in a military operation of such a scale, Beijing made it clear from the beginning that the Chinese action would be limited in both scope and duration, that China did not want "a single inch" of Vietnamese territory, and that Chinese troops would be withdrawn as soon as they had administered the punishment Vietnam deserved and accomplished their mission.[147] Similar statements were made at least three times in the course of the hostilities, including one on February 25 – at the height of the war – by Vice Premier Wang Chen, who told British journalists that Chinese troops would not move on to the Red River Delta or toward Hanoi itself. Chinese troops did in fact withdraw behind the prewar borderline by mid-March of 1979.[148]

Although the possibility of Soviet military intervention clearly curtailed Beijing's freedom of action, the brevity of the incursion and the unusual degree of self-restraint China exercised, in contrast to the scale of the invasion and the intensity of fighting, also suggest that the Chinese invasion had been intended to serve a larger purpose as well. By rapidly dealing the Vietnamese a major military blow, China apparently sought to demonstrate to Hanoi China's determination to defend its territorial integrity at all costs without at the same time shutting the door to negotiations. Prolonging the hostilities or allowing them to escalate into an all-out war might well permanently strain the Sino-Vietnamese relations. By demonstrating China's ability to seize and occupy Vietnamese territory at will without, however, actually doing so, Beijing hoped to pressure Hanoi into reconsidering its position vis-à-vis China in the territorial dispute and achieve a breakthrough in the stalled negotiations. For China to seize any disputed territory, which, after all, was insignificant in size, or to occupy Vietnamese territory would not only lend credence to Hanoi's charges of Chinese expansionism but could well harden Hanoi's position on the offshore islands — particularly the Spratlies — over which China was unable to exercise sovereignty and which could only be resolved through negotiations.

China's eagerness to talk to Vietnam again was indicated in that Beijing proposed negotiations immediately after the invasion began and at least three times during the war and made concrete proposals as soon as the armed conflict ended in mid-March.[149] China's intention became clear to all even before the hostilities were over, when Vice Premier Li Xiannian, in an interview with Japanese reporters on March 5, made it known that China was "ready to make concessions on the contested land areas if Vietnam was reasonable on other territorial issues," that is, on the demarcation of the Gulf of Tonkin and the ownership of the South China Sea islands.[150]

As it turned out, the Chinese were too optimistic in their calculations. Whatever "lesson" the Chinese had originally intended to teach the Vietnamese was seriously undermined by the limited nature of the military operation and all the explicit references to self-restraint on the Chinese part. Precisely because China's invasion was both short lived and confined to well-defined limits and yet was aimed at achieving larger objectives the attainment of which was beyond its military power, it could not have convinced Vietnam of China's ability to exert effective pressure or of Hanoi's need to change its own position on any issues under dispute. That China paid nearly as high a price as Vietnam in the war in terms of casualties only further reduced the credibility of Beijing's military threat. Moreover, the swift and complete withdrawal of all Chinese troops removed whatever little leverage China might have gained during the war. By making Vietnam the apparent victim of Chinese aggression and by inflicting considerable casulties and damages on Vietnam, the border war added a new emotional dimension to the already intractable territorial dispute. While China did not acquire any new bargaining power as a result of the war, Vietnam was more determined than ever to hold onto its gains.

5

The Continuing Debate

When Hanoi finally agreed to talk to China once again in April 1979, the positions of the two sides were as far apart as ever. At the first plenary session of the peace talks held on April 18, Vietnam presented a three-point proposal for the settlement of the problems in Sino-Vietnamese relations. The first point, which apparently commanded the top priority from Hanoi's point of view, contained the following "urgent measures for guaranteeing security, peace, and stability in the border areas": (1) The two sides should stop all acts of war provocation and all forms of hostile activities that violate the sovereignty and territorial integrity of each other or threaten its security; (2) The two countries should refrain from concentrating troops along their common border and pull back their armed forces into their own territory to a distance of three to five kilometers from the lines of actual control prior to the border war; and (3) A demilitarized zone should be created for the area where no armed forces were present and a joint commission set up to supervise the cease-fire. The second point proposed the normalization of relations between the two countries on the basis of "respect for independence, sovereignty, and territorial integrity; nonaggression, refraining from the use of force or the threat of use of force, noninterference in the internal affairs of the other side."

The third point, specifically directed at the disputed land territory, reaffirmed Hanoi's previous stand by proposing that the dispute be settled on the principle of "respect for the status quo of the borderline left by history and delineated by the 1887 and 1895 conventions."[151]

Hanoi obviously was preoccupied with the issue of the land border. The only indirect reference made to the South China Sea was a suggestion to settle all disputes "in a spirit of mutual respect and mutual benefit," which apparently meant that Vietnam still wanted to share these islands more or less equally with China.[152] Presumably satisfied with the status quo in the South China Sea for the time being and realizing China's inability to seize the Spratlies in the near future, the Vietnamese appeared to show little interest in any issue except that of forestalling new military incursions from the north. Even here, their insistence on the establishment of the demilitarized zone on the basis of the prewar boundary was tantamount to demanding Chinese recognition of the status quo that was still in Vietnam's favor.

The Chinese, on the other hand, were clearly more ambitious. At the second session of the talks, Beijing put forth an eight-point proposal that covered all the outstanding issues of bilateral conflict, including the ethnic Chinese in Vietnam and the situation in Kampuchea. Out of the eight points, however, three concerned the territorial dispute, indicating its prominence in Chinese thinking. Moreover, the Chinese intended to discuss and settle all three areas of the territorial dispute. With regard to the border, Beijing reiterated the stand it had always taken, that the land boundary "as delimited by the Sino-French boundary accords" should be respected and serve as a basis for a negotiated settlement and that, before such a settlement, the status quo of the borderline since 1958 should be maintained.

With regard to the sea areas and islands in the South China Sea, Beijing proposed that the two sides demarcate their respective economic zones and continental shelves in both the Gulf of Tonkin and other sea areas "in a fair and reasonable way" and in accordance with the relevant principles of the existing international law. Obviously, China had in mind the "median line" principle according to which a boundary would be drawn more or less parallel and equidistant to the coastlines of the two nations. As far as the Paracels and the Spratlies were concerned, however, Beijing insisted that they had always been "an inalienable part of Chinese territory." Hanoi should therefore return to its previous position, recognizing and respecting China's sovereignty over these two island groups and withdrawing all its personnel from the Spratlies.[153]

From the beginning, the two countries focused their attention on different issues, and the negotiations served quite different purposes for them. Having been attacked by China and being unsure of its next move, Vietnam naturally sought assurances against another Chinese invasion. Vietnam contended that, because the Chinese invasion constituted the fundamental cause of tension along the entire border, the first order of business for the bilateral talks was to prevent a renewal of hostilities. Until peace and stability in the border areas could be guaranteed, there was no point in discussing other issues relevant to the two countries.[154] Hence Vietnam insisted that the first point of its proposal be given top priority and even put forth a draft agreement for immediate signature by both sides that would require the two countries to refrain from offensive activities, armed provocation, and any other activities that might endanger the security of each other.[155] For Vietnam, the border situation presented the only immediate threat from China that was worthy of any concern; only when Vietnam was secure from future Chinese attacks could Hanoi regain any bargaining power with regard to other larger territorial issues.

China, on the other hand, contended that the border war was a symptom, not a cause, if the woeful state of Sino-Vietnamese relations and that the potential for renewed hostilities between the two could be eliminated and the land border stabilized only when other larger issues were resolved.[156] Thus China refused to discuss demilitarization or other specific measures related to border security unless Hanoi renounced its hegemonistic designs in the region and its claims to Chinese territory. With the border situation more or less under control after the punitive action against Vietnam and with a large concentration of Chinese troops along the border, Beijing apparently believed that it was time to discuss larger territorial and regional issues that could best be settled through negotiations and hoped that Hanoi would now be more amenable. Indeed, while a continuing show of force along the border was necessary for China to achieve other objectives beyond the land border, it was also the only way of effectively exerting pressure upon Vietnam. To agree to Vietnam's proposal before anything significant was accomplished on these larger issues would simply be to tie China's own hands and defeat the purpose of the costly military operation that it had just undertaken.

In the light of the above, it is no wonder that this new round of negotiations, just like the two previous ones, was a futile exercise, and the negotiating hall was soon turned into a forum for accusations and counteraccusations. In refusing to discuss the Vietnamese three-point proposal, China was repeatedly accused of shunning the responsibility for its "criminal war against the Vietnamese people" and obstructing the progress of the talks.[157] By insisting on discussing its own eight-point proposal and by raising larger issues not immediately relevant to the border situation, China was displaying its "big-nation expansionism and hegemonism."[158] Moreover, by demanding Vietnamese recognition of Chinese sovereignty over the South China Sea islands immediately after launching a war of aggression against Vietnam, China exposed its "designs to annex step by step" the entire South China Sea.[159]

Vietnam, by insisting on the reduction of border tension without first agreeing to examine the causes of such tension and by making a supervised cease-fire along the land border the precondition of any meaningful talk, was accused by China of evading the real substantive issues of dispute.[160] At a time when Vietnam was accelerating its anti-Chinese activities and its military operation in Kampuchea, Hanoi's proposal for demilitarization along the Sino-Vietnamese border was nothing but "a trick to hoodwink world public opinion" and a "camouflage" to cover up its hegemonistic deeds in Indochina.[161] As Vietnam would discuss nothing but the border issue, while China would discuss anything but that issue, the negotiations never got off the ground. Although a total of 15 sessions were held over a span of nearly one year, no progress was made on any substantive issue. The only accomplishment concerned the exchange of prisoners of war. The talks were finally called off, this time by China, in March 1980.

While the negotiations were stalled by a basic disagreement over procedural matters, claims and counterclaims over territorial issues continued with increasing vigor outside the negotiating hall. The two sides took pains to dig up new evidence to substantiate their claims to the South China Sea islands, which now became the focus of the continuing debate. On July 30, 1979, the Chinese delegation to the second round of peace talks, held in Beijing, distributed to foreign reporters a pamphlet entitled "Some Documents and Materials Concerning the Vietnamese Government's Recognition of the Xisha and Nansha Islands as Chinese Territory." The pamphlet made public for the first time facsimiles of statements made by Pham Van Dong on September 14, 1958 and Hanoi's endorsement of the Chinese declaration of May 9, 1965, as well as maps and Vietnamese text books published between 1960 and 1974, to show that Vietnam itself had recognized Chinese sovereignty over the two archipelagoes.[162]

Without denying the existence of these documents, the Vietnamese Foreign Ministry in a series of rebuttals contended that China had distorted the "letter and spirit" of the 1958 statement that was meant to apply only to the 12-mile territorial sea and that the 1965 Vietnamese statement must be viewed against the "historical background" of the difficult struggle against U.S. imperialism.[163] In a statement made on August 12, Hanoi further claimed that the Chinese had "misused the Vietnamese trust in the process of printing a number of Vietnamese maps [during the war] by drawing the map signs on some border sections deeper into Vietnamese territory, thus annexing some parts of Vietnam." This was why on some Vietnamese maps the Paracels and Spratlies were included in Chinese territory.[164] Hanoi also claimed some of the documents China presented on Vietnam's recognition of Chinese ownership of the two island groups were fabrications.[165]

In a long article entitled "Hoang Sa Archipelago" published in September, Hanoi for the first time made a case against China's claims to the Paracels, about which it had hitherto kept relatively quiet. Hanoi contended that the entire archipelago was discovered by the Vietnamese "very long ago" and had been controlled by them "ever since."[166] Citing from some Vietnamese and some foreign sources, Hanoi claimed that Vietnam as early as the seventeenth century had begun to exploit the archipelago and levy taxes on foreign fishing boats operating in the islands. The fact that the "Paracels" had been named after Vietnam's central coast known to foreign navigators as "Costa de Pracel" was sufficient to show that the archipelago had long been recognized as part of Vietnam.[167] In the same article, Vietnam also proceeded to refute Chinese claims based upon archeological finds that had been made from time to time. Without challenging the presence of ancient Chinese cultural relics on the Paracels, Hanoi argued that archeological finds merely indicated the "cultural interflow" between China and other countries. As such, the presence of these relics on the Paracels was no more sufficient to validate China's claims of sovereignty over the archipelago than the presence of similar finds or the presence of ethnic Chinese in Vietnam and other Asian countries would be to any Chinese claim of sovereignty over these nations. Indeed, in view of the "many wars of aggression" conducted by China against Vietnam throughout history, the discovery on Vietnamese territory of traces of China's age-old hegemonism was no surprise. As such, it certainly played "no role in determining the sovereignty of the archipelago."[168]

In a statement made by Vietnam's Foreign Ministry on September 27, 1979, Hanoi claimed that Vietnam's sovereignty over both the Paracels and the Spratlies was "incontestable," and it possessed "all the juridical, historical, and realistic facts to prove this unquestionable truth."[169] Such "facts" were soon to come. On September 28, Hanoi released a White Paper entitled "Vietnam's Sovereignty on the Hoang Sa and Truong Sa Archipelago" that contained 19 documents dating back to the seventeenth century. Made up of official chronicles, maps, and colonial ordinances, these documents purportedly showed that Vietnam was the first in history officially to survey, exploit, occupy, claim ownership of, and exercise sovereignty over both archipelagoes. Hanoi now claimed that Vietnam had discovered these islands in the seventeenth century and that the imperial court of Annam officially established sovereignty over the Paracels as early as 1816 with an occupation. Up to that time, no other country had challenged Vietnam's sovereignty or had tried to establish its own. A detailed chronicle of events was also included to show how Vietnam had exercised "de facto and de jure control" through repeated annexations by successive regimes and official declarations over the last two centuries.[170]

To counter the Vietnamese claims, China, on January 30, 1980, published an even longer document entitled "China's Indisputable Sovereignty over the Xisha and Nansha Islands" that contained documents and data dating back as early as the third century A.D. Quoting from these historical records, Beijing contended that the Chinese discovered the two archipelagoes in the second century B.C. and had begun to inhabit them as early as the seventh century. By the tenth century, Chinese naval patrols had reached the Xisha Islands and placed them under Chinese jurisdiction. In the ensuing centuries, the Chinese government continued to conduct surveys around the islands and dispatch naval patrols to their adjacent areas. To further strengthen its legal position, Beijing also produced both imperial and foreign maps, atlases, and encyclopedias to show that not only had the Chinese government repeatedly asserted its sovereignty over the islands in recent times, but also the two island groups had long been recognized as Chinese territory in the international community.[171] Because China had owned these islands before the twentieth century, their seizure by France in 1933 was an act of aggression that could not establish sovereign rights for Vietnam nor in any way change the legal status of the archipelagos as Chinese territory.[172] What was most important, Beijing argued, was that there had been no dispute over the islands before 1974 because the Vietnamese government itself had repeatedly recognized China's sovereignty. Hanoi's recent departure from its original position was therefore something "absolutely impermissable under international law."[173]

To pursue the matter further, in the same document and in a series of articles published in 1980 Beijing produced evidence showing that China had given names to the major islands in both the Paracels and the Spratlies as early as the Sung Dynasty (960–1297 A.D.) and that Chinese navigators by the eighteenth century at the latest had already identified more than 70 islands in the Spratly group and more than 30 islands in the Paracel group. Moreover, the foreign names given to some of these islands in later centuries – for example, Paxo (by the Portuguese in the eighteenth century) in the Paracel group, Sincoe, Namyit (both by the English in the nineteenth century), and Itu Aba (by the Japanese in the twentieth century) in the Spratly group were in fact all transliterations of long-existing Chinese names.[174]

To refute Vietnam's claims further, China proceeded to show in great detail that the specific islands Hanoi had claimed to have discovered in the seventeenth century and occupied in 1816 were geographically, topographically, and ecologically not part of the Paracels or the Spratlies but some offshore islands closer to the coast of central Vietnam.[175] Citing new passages from both Chinese and Vietnamese sources that contained similar descriptions of the same islands referred to by Hanoi, Beijing managed to produce corroborating evidence showing that the terms Hoang Sa and Truong Sa in Vietnam's historical records were in fact the present Ly Son Dao and Chiem Ba Dao archipelagos lying parallel but close to the Vietnamese coast and could not possibly be part of either the Paracels or the Spratly group that lie hundreds of miles off Vietnam.[176] Beijing contended the word "Paracels" mentioned in Western history books before 1820s referred precisely to these offshore islands of Vietnam, because it had been explicitly defined to cover the area from longitude 109°10′ to 111° east and latitude 12° to 17° north, which is one to three degrees to the west of the present Paracels. It was not until after that time that the term came to refer specifically to both such islands and China's Xisha — eventually in the latter part of the nineteenth century to the Xisha alone.[177] Therefore, in insisting that "Truong Sa" and "Hoang Sa" were identical to the Paracels and the Spratlies from the beginning, Hanoi had deliberately distorted history.[178]

In a long, follow-up article published on December 2, 1980, Beijing also described the Vietnamese position on the Gulf of Tonkin as "fantastic" and "legally untenable." Referring to the relevant maps of the Sino-French boundary conventions, China pointed out that the red line drawn on the Gulf of Tonkin extended only as far as latitude 21°23″ north from the eastern end of the Sino-Vietnamese land border — not even one-seventh of the length of the gulf, which, after all, was not mentioned by the treaties at all and only partially included on the map. China therefore contended that the delineation of the gulf was neither the letter nor the intent of the treaties and that the French version of the provision, which diverged from the Chinese, could only mean a line of demarcation determining the ownership of the islands in the sea.[179] Beijing argued that a boundary line without a terminal point could not possibly be a boundary line as such, and if Hanoi was to construe the red line as a boundary line, there was no reason why it should be extended only up to the Vietnamese coast at around 17° north rather than beyond it and across the entire southern part of Vietnam. Beijing also demonstrated that in the process of rather prolonged negotiations between China and France in the nineteenth century, the two sides only fought over the ownership of a few controversial offshore islands, never over the water area of the gulf. The word "boundary" in the French version could only mean a line of demarcation determining the ownership of the islands in the gulf.[180]

China argued that under international law the Gulf of Tonkin had an outlet far too wide for it to be a historical gulf, and it had never been recognized or treated as such by the international community or any maritime power, France included. Even more important, China pointed out that Hanoi, in the three fishery agreements signed with China in 1957, set 12 nautical miles from the coasts of the two countries as the limit of their jurisdiction, leaving the remainder of the gulf as a common fishing zone. Again, in September 1964, when Hanoi announced its 12-mile territorial sea, a line delineating the Vietnamese territorial sea in the Gulf of Tonkin was clearly drawn on an accompanying map. Therefore, neither China nor Vietnam – or France before it – had ever exercised or intended to exercise full sovereignty over the entire gulf.[181] To insist that the gulf had long been delineated or that both nations had exercised sovereignty over it was therefore to impose the concept of present-day law of the seas on an old treaty, which was nothing less than fabricating history.[182]

On January 18, 1982, Vietnam's Foreign Ministry released a second White Paper on territorial matters entitled "The Hoang Sa and Truong Sa Archipelagoes: Vietnamese Territories," which contained even more historical documents, including administrative decrees, testimonies of Western navigators, and books on history and geography. The book showed not only that the "Hoang Sa" and "Truong Sa" indeed referred to a large sea area of small islands and sandbanks far out in the South China Sea, but also that the Vietnamese state had exercised "long-standing and uninterrupted sovereignty" over the Paracels and the Spratlies.[183] Specifically, the book produced detailed information showing how the imperial court of Annam had repeatedly and regularly exploited the two archipelagoes in the eighteenth and nineteenth centuries. It described at great length how France had "carried on the exercise of sovereignty" over these islands on behalf of the Vietnamese state during the colonial era.[184] A chronicle of events showed how the Saigon regime had effectively "exercised and defended" Vietnam's sovereignty over the two archipelagoes in the postwar period through official annexations of these island groups, erection of stone markers, declarations at international conferences, and protests against claims made by foreign governments.[185] Because the imperial court of Annam, the French colonial government, and the Saigon regime had all acted in the name of the Vietnamese state when they made claims to or attempted to assert sovereignty over the islands, Hanoi implied that China should not merely rely upon Hanoi's words and actions for evidence.[186]

To refute China's charges of misrepresentation, Hanoi argued that the terms "Hoang Sa" and "Truong Sa" had long existed in Vietnam's historical records, whereas the words "Xisha" and "Nansha" had been coined by China only in the twentieth century. If Hoang Sa and Truong Sa were not the Paracels and the Spratlies, then Xisha and Nansha were even less so.[187] Hanoi also contended that some of the islands referred to in the historical documents produced by Beijing were offshore islands of China's Guangdong Province and Hainan Island, not part of the Paracels or the Spratlies.[188] "Even if it is true that the Chinese discovered these archipelagoes," Hanoi argued, mere discovery could not constitute a legal basis for Chinese claims and "in no way help create sovereign rights" for China.[189] Hanoi contended that the historical documents cited by China were mostly "writings recording contemporary Chinese cognizance of geographical positions, history, and customs of foreign countries in Southeast Asia" and that explorations of these islands by the Chinese throughout the centuries were made by private citizens and therefore were not official acts of the state.[190] Because China had never "actually taken possession" of these islands until the twentieth century and had never challenged the Vietnamese exercise of sovereignty over them before then, the landing of Chinese troops on the Paracels in 1909, the occupation of the Itu Aba Island in the Spratly group and Ile Boisée (i.e., Woody Island) in the Paracel group in December 1946, and the seizure of the entire Paracels in 1974 were all acts of armed aggression that could not create any rights or titles for China.[191] Indeed, China's continuing claims to and occupation of these islands after launching a massive invasion of Vietnam only showed its plan for "conquering Vietnam . . . and turning eventually the Eastern Sea [i.e., South China Sea] into a Chinese lake."[192] Hanoi therefore demanded that China return the Paracels to Vietnam and renounce all claims to both archipelagoes.[193]

On May 12, 1982, in a lengthy commentary on Vietnam's "sea areas and continental shelves," Hanoi went a step further by drawing support for its claims from a Vietnamese legend, according to which,

> Our first ancestors were born from a sac that contained 100 eggs. After their birth fifty of them followed their mother to go to the mountains while the other fifty followed their father to go toward the sea. This attests to the fact that the early Vietnamese did not confine themselves to the Red River Delta, but they also set out to conquer the mountains and the seas.[194]

Acknowledging that the Vietnamese sense of territoriality had previously been underdeveloped, it went on to proclaim "The . . . concept that Vietnam consisted only of the S-shaped continent and the Hoang Sa and Truong Sa archipelagoes has now become obsolete," because there was now an "oceanic Vietnam which is *several times larger* [italics added] than continental Vietnam," thereby claiming virtually the entire South China Sea.[195] In the same statement, Hanoi also revealed the stake Vietnam had in the continuing dispute when it declared that, in asserting Vietnam's sovereignty over the sea area around the Spratlies and the Paracels, Vietnam was not merely protecting its "rich natural resources, notably petroleum and natural gas" but also "making a practical contribution to checking Beijing's scheme of oceanic expansion."[196]

Just as in the previous cases, these new Vietnamese pronouncements did not go unchallenged in Beijing. On June 11, 1982, China, in another rebuttal, maintained that Vietnam could not possibly sustain its claim of having exercised sovereignty in the South China Sea islands by using only "ancient documentary materials." China was "the first to discover, exploit and exercise jurisdiction" over these islands, and there was no country other than China that exercised state power over these islands prior to the early 1930s.[197] Beijing went on to point out that even the French Foreign Minister Aristide Briand acknowledged in 1921 "the impossibility in which we currently find ourselves to claim these islands."[198] In 1929, the French acting governor general in Indochina also had conceded that "according to reports from various sources, the Paracels should be regarded as belonging to China."[199] France's brief occupation of the two archipelagoes in the 1930s, therefore, was clearly an act of aggression that could not bestow sovereignty. Much less could subsequent Vietnamese regimes inherit any legal titles from such occupation. Moreover, because China's claims to the South China Sea islands had been repeatedly recognized by Vietnam itself as well as by other nations before 1974, it was clearly Vietnam that had been "propelled by expansionist designs" and therefore "did not hesitate to distort history and fabricate lies." But whatever Vietnam did, it could "in no way alter historical facts and the legal basis regarding China's ownership of the two archipelagoes since ancient times."[200]

6

Toward Armed Confrontation Again?

As there seemed to be no end to the drawn out debate and no conclusive answers to the legal issues or factual questions raised in the controversy, China and Vietnam proceeded to take steps to consolidate their respective positions in the South China Sea after the 1979 war. No sooner had the war ended than China decided to speed up permanent settlement on the Paracels and to ensure effective control by moving hundreds of civilians to the archipelago, in addition to an unspecified number of ground troops.[201] On July 23, 1979, China for "considerations of safety" declared four "danger zones" covering part of the Paracels and part of the international waters and banned all aircraft from these zones indefinitely.[202] Although Beijing's proclamation professed to "concern areas within China only," the nature of such a measure clearly gave the impression that Beijing considered the entire Paracels an integral part of China and was determined to exercise exclusive control not only of the archipelago but also over the adjacent waters and air space. That such a proclamation came amidst reports of Chinese air and naval exercises conducted in the same area was no coincidence.[203] In late August, the entire Paracels were further integrated with mainland China through better communication links with the Hainan Island, when a twice-weekly air service was inaugurated.[204] By May 1980, China had already installed two new lighthouses and one air traffic guidance tower on the Paracels and set up a local government complete with new residential blocks, banks, hospitals, post offices, and other facilities.[205] In July 1981, a factory capable of desalinating 200 tons of sea water daily was also constructed, along with an apparently elaborate air defense system for the archipelago, as revealed in the publicity given to the training of antiaircraft gun units stationed there.[206] This was followed soon by another military exercise conducted around Hainan Island.[207]

In early February 1982, immediately following the release of the second Vietnamese White Book on the South China Sea islands, Generals Yang Dezhi and Yang Yong, chief and deputy chief of the PLA's General Staff, made a much publicized trip to the Paracels.[208] As Yang Dezhi had been the commander in chief of the Chinese forces during the 1979 border war, the trip was apparently calculated to show Beijing's determination to defend the islands. In June, Beijing announced the completion of a "vast harbor" by naval engineers on the southernmost tip of the Paracels on Zhongjian Island, which was in every sense a naval base, thereby increasing China's operational capabilities in the South China Sea.[209] By August 1982, the entire Paracels were designated as a restricted military zone, and Chinese forces stationed there were instructed to fire at sight at any unauthorized vessels intruding into the area.[210] As late as February 1983, another delegation led by the governor and party chief of Guangdong Province paid a visit to the Paracels to boost the morale of the troops stationed there. During the visit, publicity was given specifically to the naval units on Zhongjian Island, who pledged their determination to defend and build up the Paracels.[211]

To back up its territorial claims further, China also began to conduct seismic surveys and exploration activities around Hainan Island and in the Gulf of Tonkin as early as July 1979.[212] By September, China had awarded oil and gas exploration rights in the Gulf of Tonkin and the sea areas between Hainan Island and the Paracels to foreign companies.[213] Significantly, one of the two companies given such rights in the Gulf of Tonkin was a French firm, probably a deliberate move to obtain French acquiescence in the Chinese interpretation of the gulf.[214] In the meantime, on September 29, 1979, to prevent any other foreign countries from exploring the energy resources in the area around the distant Spratlies, which China could not yet control, Beijing once again issued a declaration that not only asserted China's "indisputable sovereignty over these islands and surrounding sea areas and the natural resources therein," but also warned that "China's lawful sovereignty over the Nansha islands brooks no infringement by any country on any pretext and by any means. . . . Encroachment upon any part of these islands and exploitative or any other activity undertaken in these areas by any foreign country are illegal and impermissable."[215] The warning was repeated many times in the ensuing years.[216] In early 1982, China opened for bidding a number of oil fields in the eastern part of the Gulf of Tonkin and south of Hainan Island.[217] By the end of the year, foreign oil companies had already started prospecting for and extracting oil and gas in these fields, and China also announced plans to conduct geological surveys around both the Paracels and the Spratlies.[218]

In April 1983, China announced the standardized names of all the 155 islands and reefs in the four archipelagoes of the South China Sea, in another attempt to bolster its claims.[219] The list was also the most exhaustive one ever published by any country. (See the appendix.) In late September, Beijing did not hesitate to condemn the reported occupation by Malaysian troops of Swallow Reef (*Danwan Jiao* in Chinese), at the southern tip of the Spratly group, as "illegal," and once again to assert China's sovereignty over the entire archipelago.[220] As late as May 1984, Beijing took the further step of establishing a separate administrative region for Hainan Island, which comprised all the South China Sea islands. Although the declared purpose of this administrative measure was to facilitate economic development of the region, the intention of the Chinese government to exercise a more effective control over the South China Sea situation was obvious.[221]

If China was eager to strengthen its posture, Vietnam also lost no time in doing the same. While China's activities were mainly centered around the Paracels, Vietnam paid more attention to the Spratlies. Almost immediately after the border war, Vietnam granted the Soviet Union the right to use Hanoi's largest naval base at Cam Ranh Bay, which led to an immediate increase of Soviet naval activity off the Vietnamese coast.[222] The invitation to the Soviets was clearly calculated to strengthen Vietnam's position vis-à-vis China in the South China Sea. At the same time, Hanoi also took measures to increase its military strength on the six Spratly islands it had occupied. By early June 1980, Vietnamese newspapers had begun to give publicity to the construction and training activities on these islands. The Vietnamese troops stationed on two of them — Sinh Ton and An Bang — were specially commended for their determination to build the Spratlies into a "steel-like archipelago" and an "impregnable [outpost] of the fatherland."[223] By May 1981, logistical support from mainland Vietnam to the six Spratly islands was reported to have improved to ensure an uninterrupted supply of large quantities of goods to the troops stationed there.[224] In August 1981, the training activity of Vietnamese naval and antiaircraft units stationed on another two Spratly islands — Quang Vinh and An Giang — was also reported, thereby suggesting a further expansion of Vietnam's defense network on the archipelago.[225]

In early February 1982, at about the time the high-ranking Chinese generals were visiting the Paracels, Marshal Nikolai V. Ogarkov, chief of the General Staff of the Soviet Armed Forces and first vice minister of defense, was also invited to lead a military delegation to Hanoi.[226] The visit was accompanied by reports on the construction of a naval base on Con Son Island, an island 60 miles off the tip of southern Vietnam, by several hundred Soviet military advisers and technicians.[227] Because the island represented the closest point from mainland Vietnam to the Spratlies, the purpose was clearly to increase the cruising range of the Vietnamese and possibly also the Soviet navies in the South China Sea.

By November 1982, a Soviet fleet of about 12 vessels was already permanently stationed in Cam Ranh Bay, with at least another dozen or so vessels operating in the South China Sea.[228] In the meantime, as if to show Hanoi's firm grip on the entire archipelago, Vietnamese troops stationed on the six islands and the Vietnamese Navy cruising in the vicinity did not hesitate to fire on all unauthorized vessels in the area, including both refugee boats and pleasure yachts.[229] Vietnam has for some time been expanding, though discreetly, its area of control in the Spratlies region, and by April 1983, Hanoi had reportedly taken control of six additional islands in the archipelago and built a paved runway, an operations building, and a control and communication tower capable of accommodating short take-off and landing aircraft of types thought to be currently in use in Vietnam.[230] By mid-June 1984, Vietnamese troops on some of the Spratly islands were reportedly already equipped with amphibious tanks, and one of the tiny islands had as many as 600 Vietnamese troops.[231]

Coupled with these activities, Hanoi, as early as 1979, also sought to explore energy resources in the South China Sea.[232] In May 1980, Hanoi awarded major rights to the Soviet Union to tap offshore oil deposits in the southern part of Vietnam's continental shelf.[233] By July, Hanoi had already entered a formal agreement with Moscow to cooperate in the exploration and exploitation of oil and gas both on Vietnam's southern continental shelf and in the area near the Spratly islands.[234] Such exploration activities increased steadily during 1981, and, by 1982, the Soviet Union had become the only foreign company assisting Vietnam in its search for oil.[235]

In the meantime, to make sure that it had at least some control of the situation in the northern part of the South China Sea and in the Gulf of Tonkin, Hanoi from late 1979 on also took the trouble to reiterate its claims every time there was a new development in these areas. Thus, on September 3, 1979, Vietnam charged that China's enclosure of four "dangerous zones" near the Paracels was a "brazen violation" of

Vietnam's territorial integrity over the airspace and waters of the Hoang Sa archipelago.[236] On September 27, 1979, only one day after Beijing reasserted its claims of sovereignty over the South China Sea islands, Hanoi declared "Any activities by any foreign countries to occupy, to try to occupy, explore, survey, and exploit Hoang Sa and Truong Sa . . . will be illegal."[237] The same warning was repeated in January 1980, when China stepped up its surveying activities in the area of the Paracels. In a more sharply worded statement, Hanoi warned against "all surveys and scientific researches conducted by any foreign countries, whether they are basic surveys or surveys on the natural resources in the territorial seas, the exclusive economic zones, as well as the continental shelves of the Hoang Sa and Truong Sa archipelagoes without the agreement of the Vietnamese government." It also pledged to defend its territorial sovereignty over the natural resources in the South China Sea.[238] In May 1982, after China had announced the opening of bidding for oil fields in the southern part of the Gulf of Tonkin, Hanoi reiterated its claim to the gulf.[239] In late September 1982, immediately after China had contracted foreign companies to work in the Gulf of Tonkin, Hanoi once again declared all oil or gas prospecting and extracting activities by foreign oil companies in the eastern part of the gulf and around the Spratlies and the Paracels without Vietnamese permission as illegal.[240]

By late 1982 Vietnam also began, though belatedly, its own exploration activities in the Gulf of Tonkin.[241] On November 12, 1982, Hanoi, in announcing the baseline for determining the width of Vietnam's territorial waters, proceeded to declare unilaterally that the boundary in the Gulf of Tonkin had been delineated by the 1887 Sino-French boundary convention, and the part of the gulf belonging to Vietnam was "historical waters that fall under the internal water systems of SRV."[242] In February 1983, Hanoi once again warned that oil exploration by U.S. companies in the Gulf of Tonkin and in areas off southwest Hainan constituted a violation of Vietnamese sovereignty.[243] As late as June 1984, Hanoi protested strongly over China's incorporation of the Spratlies

and the Paracels into the newly established Hainan Administrative Region by declaring once again that the two archipelagoes were "sacred parts of Vietnamese territories," which
was "an undeniable fact that cannot be changed by any trick,
distortion, or perfidious schemes of the Peking expansion-
ists." Hanoi also warned China to "get out of" the Paracels
and "stay away from" the Spratlies, while expressing its
determination to defend all these islands.[244]

The attempts made by both countries to consolidate their
gains and secure new footholds in both the Gulf of Tonkin
and the South China Sea inevitably increased the chances of
direct confrontation at sea. As early as April 1979, China
seized a Vietnamese reconnaissance boat allegedly conducting sabotage activities in the Paracels.[245] In July 1979, a Vietnamese gunboat also fired on two foreign supply ships off
the Gulf of Tonkin, apparently in an attempt to discourage
foreign oil companies from operating in the gulf and to demonstrate Hanoi's determination to defend the portion of the gulf
it had claimed.[246] In mid-November of 1981, a major incident
occurred when four Chinese torpedo boats and "hundreds" of
Chinese fishing trawlers allegedly repeatedly intruded into
the Vietnamese waters in the Gulf of Tonkin and off the coast
of central Vietnam, apparently in the disputed sea areas.[247]
In early March, 1982, Vietnamese gunboats fired upon three
Chinese fishing trawlers operating at 107°50′ east and 17°40′
north in the Gulf of Tonkin, less than half a degree beyond
the Vietnam-claimed sea boundary in the gulf, blowing up
one of them and seizing the other two. As a result, 6 Chinese
fishermen were injured and 18 were missing.[248] A few days
later Chinese gunboats seized a Vietnamese "spy ship"allegedly operating near the Paracels, apparently in retaliation for
the Vietnamese action.[249] Three months later, in mid-June,
a similar incident occurred when Vietnam again attacked and
seized a Chinese fishing boat in the gulf.[250] In early July,
another incident took place when 14 armed Vietnamese boats
intruded into Chinese territorial waters in the Gulf of Tonkin
and clashed with Chinese fishing trawlers. According to China, the incident took place at 20° 20′ 15″ north and 108°

11′ 45″ east, which, ironically, would be within Vietnamese waters if the median line principle advocated by China is adopted for the division of the gulf, but within Chinese waters if Vietnam's position on the gulf prevails.[251]

Such incidents are to a large extent attributable to the confusion resulting from two conflicting interpretations of the boundary line in the gulf. (See Map 1.) On August 31, 1983, Vietnamese gunboats again intercepted two Chinese fishing trawlers on the high seas in the Gulf of Tonkin and robbed the fishermen of their personal belongings.[252] This was followed by another incident on September 4 when Vietnamese forces again fired at two Chinese fishing boats operating off the Chinese coast in the northern part of the gulf.[253] In mid-April 1984, in the hitherto most belligerent posture taken in the Gulf of Tonkin, Hanoi staged its first joint amphibious landing maneuver with Soviet troops on the coast of Vietnam about 145–160 kilometers south of Haiphong—right inside the Gulf of Tonkin. This occurred amidst continuing border clashes along the Sino-Vietnamese land border. During the naval exercise, a total of 600 Soviet marines participated, along with a number of Soviet reconnaissance and antisubmarine aircraft and a fleet of eight Soviet ships, including the 37 thousand-ton aircraft carrier *Kiev* and a 14 thousand-ton assault ship.[254] As if to counter the Vietnamese move, a Chinese naval fleet, made up of an undetermined number of destroyers, frigates, and supply ships, set sail in early May—the first time since 1946—toward the Spratly Islands, in an apparent show of force in the disputed archipelago.[255] Although the fleet did not sail close to or land on any of the disputed islands, it did circle around the Spratlies, leaving no doubt of the ability of the Chinese Navy to operate in the region. Immediately after completing its tour of the Spratlies, the same fleet joined other landing ships in a three-week-long amphibious exercise involving 2,000 marines around Hainan Island, further demonstrating China's determination to defend its claims in the Gulf of Tonkin and the Paracels.[256]

Although China and Vietnam appear to be moving closer

to open, armed confrontation at sea, the 800-mile-long land border has also been far from tranquil. Soon after the border war, China apparently realized the inadequacy of its military operation in persuading Hanoi to change its mind. Having completely withdrawn its troops from Vietnam without first obtaining any concessions on any territorial issues, China decided to keep up the pressure on Vietnam not only by stationing a large number of troops along the border but also by threatening to use them against Vietnam again. Thus, in early May 1979, Deng Xiaoping told visiting UN Secretary General Dr. Kurt Waldheim that China "reserves the right to act and will teach Vietnam another lesson" if Hanoi should renew its armed provocations against China.[257] The threat was repeated by Li Xiannian in early July and by other Chinese officials many times in the following two years.[258] Since the end of the war, Beijing has not hesitated to launch attacks whenever necessary and certainly has made it a rule to respond to every single Vietnamese armed provocation with counterattacks.[259]

With China determined to use force against Vietnam, Hanoi has by no means displayed any sign of weakness and is equally prepared to take up the challenge. As soon as the 1979 war was over, Vietnam dispatched a large number of its crack troops and some of the most sophisticated weapons to the border in preparation for renewal of hostilities. By April 1979 the northern frontier had been turned into a gigantic military base.[260] Vietnam clearly revealed its determination to confront China on the battlefield in August 1979 when Hanoi openly warned China to "think twice before launching another invasion" and declared that "Vietnam would not be taken by surprise this time."[261] Having raised the already high cost of a second attack, Vietnam also has not refrained from launching small-scale attacks and counterattacks against China.

Although the border situation after 1979 was increasingly intertwined with the war in Kampuchea, the armed conflict apparently served a useful purpose in the continuing territorial dispute. Neither side could afford to soften its position without undermining its stand on the larger issues. For China, a certain amount of pressure was necessary if only to lend credibility to its threat to teach Vietnam a second lesson. Because the Sino-Vietnamese border was the only place where China could strike Vietnam effectively, China simply could not afford to appear soft on Vietnam until Hanoi made concessions on the South China Sea islands. By continuing to pressure Vietnam along the border, Beijing hopes to deter Hanoi from any further military adventure in the Paracels or the Spratlies. For Vietnam, until China made concessions on the Gulf of Tonkin and on the Spratlies, Hanoi needed to defy China on the border to retain a free hand in the South China Sea. By keeping the tension along the border high, Hanoi could presumably also expect to lend credence to its charges about China's ambitions and prove to the world China's military designs against Vietnam. Only by presenting an adamant posture could Vietnam regain meaningful bargaining power in any further negotiations on territorial matters.

As a result, border incidents broke out again almost as soon as the war ended formally in March 1979 and have in fact become increasingly violent. Accusations of armed provocations and intrusions for the purpose of sabotage, land grabbing, and even psychological warfare were made almost constantly throughout 1979 and have been commonplace since then. During the six months following the end of the border war, Hanoi charged that China had committed more than 1,000 armed provocations in violation of Vietnamese territory, killing or wounding more than 100 Vietnamese.[262] By mid-February 1981, 4,000 Chinese provocations had been committed against Vietnam.[263] From the Chinese side came accusations that Vietnam had made more than 370 military incursions into China's border regions from August to October of 1979 alone.[264] And in the 14 months following the war, Vietnam allegedly instigated more than 2,000 incidents, resulting in the death of 240 Chinese civilians and border guards.[265]

Whereas the earlier border incidents had involved relatively small infantry units of company level and shooting incidents, the clashes after the 1979 war, and particularly after 1980, often took the form of artillery duels and involved battalion or even regiment-sized units numbering several thousand men on each side. The first such large-scale artillery exchange occurred in July 1980, and a similar one took place in November 1980 when the two sides clashed for several days.[266] But the fiercest and most prolonged fighting took place in mid-1981 when the two sides engaged several thousand troops and fought almost continuously for two months from May to July over a few hills in the Fakashan area of China's Guangxi region less than one square meter in area that Vietnam had reportedly seized. During the fighting, tanks were used for the first time since the war and more than 20 thousand artillery shells were fired. As a result, both sides suffered hundreds of casualties.[267] In January 1982, another major armed clash along the land border was reported throughout the Spring Festival.[268] Since then, violent incidents have remained a recurrent phenomenon.[269]

In spring 1983, a new series of intensive armed clashes again led to a large-scale artillery duel in mid-April that lasted for three days and resulted in heavy casualties and property damage on both sides.[270] The armed conflict along the border acquired a new momentum after that, with a succession of intensive clashes taking place in August and September of 1983 and again in January 1984.[271] In late March 1984, a major incident took place when Chinese antiaircraft gunners damaged a Vietnamese MiG-21 reportedly intruding into the Guangxi border area.[272] The clashes reached a new peak in April and May 1984, when Chinese and Vietnamese troops once again engaged each other in fierce artillery exchange and ground fighting almost continuously for two months, resulting in heavy casualties and property damage for both sides.[273] During the sustained fighting, Chinese troops proceeded to seize a couple of hilltops that China claimed to be inside Chinese territory but which had been occupied by Vietnam since the war and repeatedly used to shell Chinese border villages for five straight years.[274] This action apparently triggered the unprecedented division-level attack launched by Vietnam against China in early July, in an attempt to recapture the strategic high grounds that Hanoi claimed were inside Vietnamese territory.[275]

By late November 1984, the two sides continued to exchange heavy artillery fire in several populated border areas, making it impossible for the border residents to carry on a normal life.[276] As late as April 1985, China reported that the Vietnamese troops had not "ceased firing artillery shots on Chinese targets for a single day" ever since the 1979 border war.[277] Judging from the scale and frequency of such border clashes alone, the territorial dispute has actually deepened.

7

Problems and Prospects

This survey of the nature and evolution of the Sino-Vietnamese territorial dispute reveals the complexity surrounding the three areas of conflict. The dispute is unique in at least two important ways, however. First, the whole controversy centers around a small number of land areas along a quite well defined and for a long time friendly boundary and over tiny, barren islands in the immense South China Sea over which neither side had attempted to establish effective control until recent decades. Judging from the long-standing comradeship and close cooperation between the two nations, any territorial dispute of such nature and scope should have been at least amenable to compromise and resolution. It would certainly not have brought a different pair of nations to war so abruptly.

Second, and perhaps more important, no territorial dispute existed between Hanoi and Beijing before 1974, as the two sides were almost in complete agreement on all the major issues. It was mainly a change of attitude and policy on the part of Hanoi toward the end of the Vietnam War that generated the controversy. Therefore, the territorial dispute can only reflect Hanoi's changing perceptions of itself and of China at a time when the political situation and alliance pattern in the region was undergoing a subtle but definitive transformation. The relative ease with which Hanoi turned its China policy upside down from one of support and subordination into one of challenge and intransigence clearly signifies an anxious but historical desire by Vietnam not only to reassert its independence from China after the final impetus for an alliance had been removed but also to attain its long-cherished status as a major power in the region.

If, from the Vietnamese perspective, it was only natural and desirable to move away from China when their partnership was no longer vital to the security of Vietnam, Beijing could not help but view Hanoi's rapid policy reorientation with misgivings. Nevertheless, had Hanoi avoided or at least postponed an open confrontation with Beijing on the territorial matters, China would probably have tolerated Vietnam's tilt away from China with more grace. Unfortunately this did not happen. Indeed, in the eyes of Beijing, Hanoi's drive as early as 1973 to legalize the status quo on the border, which included territories not sanctioned by the Sino-French boundary accords, was unbecoming enough, but its explicit desire to incorporate two-thirds of the Gulf of Tonkin as part of Vietnamese territorial waters in early 1974, more than a year before the end of the Vietnam War, was clearly an unfriendly, greedy act. Vietnam's outright seizure of six Spratly islands in 1975, even before the capture of Saigon, and its eagerness to claim sovereignty over the South China Sea islands immediately afterward, in spite of its previous recognition of the Chinese title to them, certainly betrayed its territorial ambitions. Hanoi's adamancy during the high-level negotiations in 1977 on all issues of dispute and the subsequent border tension, culminating in the exodus of ethnic Chinese and the long series of armed clashes in 1978, further demonstrated the extent to which Vietnam was prepared to go to realize its goals.

Indeed, with the benefit of hindsight, the early emergence of the territorial dispute, the speed of Vietnam's about-face against China, and the ambitious tone of Hanoi's demands could not but raise the question of whether the entire dispute had not been somewhat deliberately played up by

Hanoi to justify its drift away from China and to achieve larger goals in Indochina. Note that the vice foreign ministerial talks on territorial matters had hardly started at the initiative of China in October 1977 than the anti-Chinese drive within Vietnam began to develop into a national campaign, leading to the large-scale expulsion of Chinese in the spring and summer of 1978. It was perhaps also no coincidence that, in spite of the small percentage of Chinese in Vietnam residing in the north and their well-settled nature, the exodus took place mainly in this area throughout 1978, which could only complicate the negotiations still under way and further exacerbate the territorial dispute.[278]

By the same token, the steadily growing tension and violence along the border in the second half of 1978 might well have also been the result of a calculated strategy to demonstrate Hanoi's anti-China stance to obtain as much Soviet military aid and political support as possible for the pending Vietnamese invasion of Kampuchea, which had been already planned. Presumably, if Vietnam had remained on friendly terms with both China and the Soviet Union, any territorial adventure or military operation Vietnam launched in Kampuchea could well have met with the disapproval of both Beijing and Moscow. Only when the campaign against Kampuchea was seen as an anti-China act designed to reduce Chinese influence in Indochina would Vietnam be sure of firm Soviet support and therefore a successful military conquest. And what could demonstrate better the pressure from the north than a heated territorial dispute with China?

Thus, contrary to the commonly held view about the Soviet role in the Sino-Vietnamese territorial dispute, the Soviet Union, rather than being the mastermind behind the scene, was most likely pulled into the dispute by Vietnam. To be sure, without Moscow's tacit approval and even active encouragement, Hanoi probably would not have broken away from Beijing so openly and violently. Nevertheless, Vietnam began to challenge China's territorial claims at a time when China was still on friendly terms with Vietnam and before Moscow decided to side openly with Hanoi on any of the issues of conflict between China and Vietnam.[279] Thus, Soviet instigation and support, though definitely a contributory factor, was not decisive – at least in the early stage of the dispute. Once Soviet backing was ensured, however, Hanoi became more confident and less restrained in dealing with China, which in turn further exacerbated the dispute.

Whatever motives Vietnam might have had in twisting the tail of the Chinese dragon, it had clearly overdone it and apparently underestimated the extent to which China would go to defend its political interests in the region and particularly its territorial integrity. Although it was not the first time that China had had a dispute over territory with neighbors, this challenge by Vietnam was clearly the most painful one. Had Vietnam been less intimately allied with China in the recent past or for a shorter time, China would probably have reacted to Vietnam's about-face with greater restraint and more diplomatic finesse. But after more than three decades of close friendship, Beijing could not help but be appalled by the sudden, drastic change in Vietnamese attitudes and shocked by Hanoi's territorial demands. After U.S. $10 billion worth of aid and enormous human sacrifice made on behalf of Vietnam throughout two Indochinese wars, Beijing simply could not tolerate such an outright betrayal by a former partner and protégé.[280] That China chose such blunt language as "teaching Vietnam a lesson" and "not letting Vietnam run wild" and did not shrink from military confrontation even at great risk to itself clearly revealed the bitterness that China felt toward a long-time ally.

Had Vietnam confined its challenge to verbal protestations within the negotiating halls, the territorial dispute most probably would not have become a direct cause of war in 1979. Hanoi's expulsion of the ethnic Chinese across the land border and the accompanying violence along the border presented a direct challenge to China's credibility to defend its territorial integrity. If China still doubted Vietnam's true intentions in the second half of 1978, Hanoi's invasion of Kampuchea, a long-time Chinese ally, conclusively attested to the magnitude of Hanoi's ambitions. Beijing's invasion of Vietnam, therefore, was designed not only to restore control over an increasingly chaotic land border, but also to put an end, once and for all, to Hanoi's territorial aggrandizement in Southeast Asia, of which the Sino-Vietnamese border dispute constituted merely one component. In a larger sense, therefore, the territorial dispute reflected a fundamental conflict between China and Vietnam over the overall postwar territorial realignment throughout the region, which Hanoi considers a matter of course but which China rejects as totally unwarranted. In this broader sense, Vietnam, not China, wanted to effect a change in the status quo.

Apart from the political purposes served and the close linkage shown with other broader regional issues, the Sino-Vietnamese territorial dispute has been further characterized by the asymmetrical relationship between the three major issues of controversy. Although much attention has been focused upon the land border, the real bone of contention is actually the South China Sea islands. The apparent incongruity between the triviality of the land area under contest and the uncompromising stance displayed by both sides on this issue is bewildering enough. China's consistent refusal to accept the principle of treating the Gulf of Tonkin as a historical gulf belonging exclusively to China and Vietnam is also at least as odd as Vietnam's dogged insistence on interpreting the Gulf of Tonkin issue in disregard of both history and the existing rules of international law. All this indicates that the dispute over the land and the Gulf of Tonkin has been to a certain extent merely a function and symptom of larger issues in contest.

The prolonged, heated debate over the South China Sea islands since the 1979 war suggests that the posture taken by both sides on the land and gulf issues and all the wrangles over them had in fact been calculated to strengthen their respective bargaining positions on the South China Sea islands and in particular to compel each other to give up its claims to the Spratlies – hence the openly expressed desire of both sides, at least at the early stages of the dispute particularly before 1979, to trade their positions on the lesser issues for clear titles to these island groups. Whereas China announced as early as March 1979 its willingness to make concessions on land territories if Vietnam would be "reasonable" on the South China Sea issues, it is not inconceivable that China might also be prepared to compromise on the gulf if Vietnam agreed to renounce all claims to the South China Sea islands – the Spratlies in particular. Thus, when China began its oil exploration activities in the Gulf of Tonkin in late 1979, it made a deliberate effort to stay away from the disputed areas by confining its activities to the area east of 108° east, the line claimed by Vietnam as the sea boundary.

Vietnam, in proposing the principle of "equality and mutual benefit" as a basis for the division of the South China Sea, presumably might also be prepared to divide the Gulf of Tonkin on "an equal and fair basis" – as China has demanded and according to the existing principles of international law – if China agreed to recognize Vietnamese sovereignty over the Spratlies. In this connection, the late start of Vietnam's oil exploration in the Gulf of Tonkin in spite of the long-proved rich oil reserves in that area, as contrasted with its eagerness to gain a head start in the southern part of the South China Sea, is perhaps also revealing.

The reasons that both China and Vietnam have focused their attention on the Spratlies do not lie merely in the vast sea area the archipelago embraces, the strategic position it occupies, and the potentially rich energy and marine resources it promises. Perhaps the most important reason is that these islands and the surrounding area have to a large extent remained a *res nullius* because of the difficulty of permanent settlement and effective occupation, and whatever claims made to the entire archipelago are yet to be substantiated beyond reasonable doubt. Some form of international recognition thus becomes the most desirable way of acquiring sovereignty. Because China and Vietnam are the two countries with the strongest claims to the South China Sea islands both historically and legally, a bilateral agreement between them is necessary not only to secure a clear title but also to silence claims already advanced by other nations in the region and preempt any new claims.

Precisely because of the importance of the Spratlies to the two nations and the high stakes involved, however, the issue has become a non-negotiable one. In fact, it may well be the unwillingness of both sides to compromise on this hard-core issue and the mutual awareness of it that has prompted them to adopt an adamant stand on the border and Gulf of Tonkin issues. As Sino-Vietnamese relations steadily deteriorated with the exodus of the Chinese and the escalating war in Kampuchea, the two sides also became further entrenched in their respective positions.

As things stand now, the territorial dispute between China and Vietnam has little prospect of an early negotiated settlement. In this connection, it is noteworthy that for more than 30 years, the Chinese government has been steadfast on territorial matters in face of all challenges and has gone to war three times to defend its territorial integrity, including twice during the darkest days of the Communist regime. If China has not shrunk from military confrontation with much more powerful neighbors over territorial matters, it can hardly be expected to retreat from a dispute with a relatively small nation like Vietnam, much less an ungrateful neighbor. On the other hand, Vietnam has also fought powerful nations almost continuously for half a century. As a zealously nationalistic and aspiring regional power with a long tradition of resisting Chinese pressure, it is also not likely to show signs of weakness. Moreover, if Vietnam dared to challenge Chinese claims even before the end of the Vietnam War when it was beset by all sorts of internal and external problems and dependent upon Chinese aid to a considerable extent, there is no reason to believe that Vietnam will make any concession now that it is united and at peace at home, enjoys the strong backing of the Soviet Union, and seems to be consolidating its control over all of Indochina.

The unwillingness of either side to compromise has been further reinforced by the clear link between the territorial dispute and other larger political issues in the region and by the emotional dimension the prolonged conflict has developed. To the extent that the entire dispute has become inextricably intertwined with the continuing war in Kampuchea, its resolution is in a large measure conditional upon, and certainly possible only after, a satisfactory settlement of the Kampuchean situation. Because Beijing now sees its territorial dispute with Hanoi as a manifestation of Vietnam's hegemonistic designs in Southeast Asia and until Vietnam changes its Kampuchean policy and its anti-Chinese stance, China considers it essential to remain firm on all the territorial issues if only to show its determination to contain Vietnam's ambitions. To do otherwise would only imply appeasement and therefore whet the appetite of the aggressor. To make sure that Vietnam pays a price for its ingratitude and greed, China cannot afford to appear soft on any of the territorial issues.

From Vietnam's perspective, Beijing's support for Kampuchea and its obstinancy in the territorial dispute is nothing less than a deliberate effort to obstruct Hanoi's drive to reassert its status as the major regional power and to slight Vietnam in Indochina. Until China ceases interfering with Indochinese affairs and recognizes Vietnam's inherent interests in that part of Southeast Asia, Hanoi has no choice but to remain adamant on the continuing territorial dispute. Having been the apparent victim of Chinese invasion, it is all the more necessary for Vietnam to show its ability to defy Chinese pressure. To do otherwise before the Kampuchean question is solved to Hanoi's satisfaction would only demonstrate Vietnam's political weakness vis-à-vis China, if not also imply Hanoi's vacillation about the status of Kampuchea.

Because the whole controversy appears to have centered around the ownership of the South China Sea islands in general and of the Spratlies in particular, until this issue is resolved, neither the land nor the gulf issues can be settled. Here again, however, both sides are likely to persist in their demands. Being the first country to discover and exploit these islands and having claimed sovereignty over both archipelagoes for many decades, China sees no reason why it should give them up now. Already in effective control of the entire Paracels, China's determination to defend them at all costs need not be doubted. Although China has not yet occupied any island in the Spratly group, its claim to the entire archipelago can be substantiated by the continuous occupation of the largest Spratly island of Itu Aba since 1946 by Taiwan – the latter from Beijing's viewpoint being an integral part of China. Indeed, Beijing believes that, in addition to historical grounds, the Taiwanese occupation of Itu Aba has given China a legally stronger claim to the entire archipelago than that of Vietnam.[281] As long as Taiwan has no desire to give up the island nor any intention to declare itself an independent new state, Beijing need not worry about its claims being completely invalidated.

As an emerging regional power with an equally impressive historical right to the South China Sea islands, Vietnam considers it only natural to have at least a share of them. Unable to regain control of the Paracels without a major war with China, sovereignty over the Spratlies has now become Vietnam's minimum demand. Already in effective control of a dozen or so Spratly islands and knowing China's inability to seize them in the near future, Hanoi also sees no need to alter the status quo in the South China Sea. Vietnam believes that time is on its side and the problem ahead is how to prolong its occupation of the dozen or so Spratly islands and how to expand its area of control.

For all the above reasons, the positions taken by the two countries on the territorial dispute have toughened in recent years. If there had been a chance of some kind of compromise before 1979, such a possibility no longer exists today. While Vietnam's stance on the land territory and the Gulf of Tonkin has never changed since the dispute began, its position on the offshore islands has steadily hardened over the years. From suggesting a division of the South China Sea islands on the basis of mutual benefit and equality in 1977, to claiming all of them as "inviolable parts of Vietnam" after the 1979 border war, and eventually to laying claims to the entire South China Sea area and taking concrete steps to fortify the

Vietnam-occupied Spratly islands in the early 1980s, Hanoi clearly showed its determination to stay in the conflict. From gradually expanding its areas of control in the Spratly archipelago to staging a naval exercise in the Gulf of Tonkin in 1984, Hanoi has in fact been gaining new strength and new confidence in confronting China at sea.

Although before 1980 China had tried persistently to resolve the dispute through negotiations and had actually initiated both rounds of high-level talks with Vietnam, since then Beijing has consistently refused to resume negotiations with Hanoi without first seeing some evidence that Vietnam is willing to negotiate sincerely. Moreover, if China were preoccupied in the past with the Paracels, its recent sea maneuvers around Hainan Island and the show of force in the Spratly archipelago suggest that China, having acquiesced to the Vietnamese adventures in that region long enough, is now prepared to face the Vietnamese challenge in the southern part of the South China Sea. Indeed, as a result of the heated public debate and the rattling of sabers since 1979, both sides appear to have invested so much both in rhetoric and in deeds that they are now somehow inadvertently committed to the defense of their respective positions. The continuing and deepening border conflict in the past few years and the gathering clouds over the South China Sea are only the most visible manifestations of the determination of both sides to confront each other militarily as well as politically.

The slim chances for a negotiated settlement clearly suggest more armed conflict in the years to come, and the potential for renewed hostilities is by no means slight. So far, the border has been the scene of almost continuous violent incidents, but because the South China Sea islands in fact constitute the central focus of the contest, future clashes are bound to take place more and more frequently at sea. Because the Spratlies are not only what has attracted the Vietnamese attention but are also the only area of conflict in which Vietnam enjoys a clear edge over China in geography and military strength and where it could act with some impunity, Viet-

nam may well attempt to seize more islands in this archipelago. In fact, unless Vietnam does so, its claims to the entire archipelago will remain weak and may become weaker
with the passage of time. Having already beefed up its military strength along the land border to a level of parity with
China, Vietnam now should also feel freer to explore in the
South China Sea. It appears that this is probably going to
be the case if and when Vietnam consolidates its control in
Kampuchea.

To what extent Vietnam would pursue this course of action remains to be seen, but because the single biggest ob-
stacle to Hanoi's attempt to assert its claim is the continuous
occupation by the Taiwanese troops of Itu Aba, Vietnam, in
the process of buttressing its position in the Spratlies, would
sooner or later come into confrontation with the Taiwanese.
Presumably, because of logistical problems, Taiwan, with a
small armed contingent on the island, would have difficulty
in defending the island against a massive Vietnamese assault.
Vietnam's recent steady build up of its forces in the larger
Spratly islands and its quiet expansion of its control to other
islands in the archipelago, in addition to having made the two
naval bases in Danang and Cam Ranh Bay available to the
Soviet warships and to having constructed a new naval base
on Con Son Island 60 miles off the mouth of the Mekong
River, can all be seen as signs of its intention to gradually
take over control of the entire archipelago.

China, on the other hand, has so far stayed clear of any-
one of the disputed Spratly islands in spite of its rhetoric to
the contrary. This is not only because Beijing still lacks the
naval power to embark upon a military expedition distant
from its coastal line, but also because a Chinese military
operation in the Spratly area might well have serious political
repercussions on Beijing's relations with other Southeast
Asian states. Moreover, any naval activity Beijing conducted
in the area of the main Spratly islands would most likely lead
to an armed confrontation with Taiwan, which could only
weaken Chinese claims to the entire archipelago and therefore

benefit Vietnam and other coastal states claiming sovereignty over various parts of it.

But China cannot acquiesce in a prolonged Vietnamese occupation of as many as a dozen Spratly islands, much less a further expansion of Vietnamese control of the archipelago, without seriously undermining its own claim of sovereignty over this island group. Yet as long as Vietnam refuses to give up the dozen or so Vietnam-occupied islands and China lacks sufficient naval forces to recapture them, the only convenient alternative to a negotiated settlement would be for China to exert pressures along the Sino-Vietnamese land border. If Vietnam should attempt to occupy more Spratly islands, there is bound to be a further escalation of the border tension into large-scale clashes. Indeed, the steadily rising scale of the armed clashes between China and Vietnam may well have been closely linked to the growing tension, if not also the gradually changing balance of forces in the South China Sea. At any rate, apart from serving as an important barometer of the military situation in Kampuchea, the land border situation will remain an index of the development of the territorial dispute over the South China Sea islands.

How far China would tolerate any further Vietnamese adventures in the South China Sea without similar countermeasures is difficult to predict. As long as Hanoi keeps away from Itu Aba, which is the symbol of China's claim to the entire archipelago, Beijing will probably refrain from launching a naval attack in the area, although certain measures could and might well be taken against some offshore islands of Vietnam in the Gulf of Tonkin or off central Vietnam in retaliation. Much certainly also depends upon the nature and effectiveness of Taiwan's responses to such Vietnamese advances. As long as Taiwan is both determined and able to defend the main islands in the archipelago, Beijing would find it unnecessary to take any concrete action.[282] But once Hanoi decides to seize Itu Aba, and, moreover, if Taiwanese troops should prove unable to hold on to it, Beijing would find it impossible to stand idly by. Under these circumstances, a seaborne Chinese military expedition is probably a foregone conclusion. In this connection, the rapid development of the Paracels as a naval base and the recent cruise of a Chinese naval fleet around the Spratlies has been apparently aimed at preparing China for such an eventuality.

In the event of an armed confrontation between China and Vietnam in the South China Sea, the Soviet Navy probably would not intervene in a showdown between China and Vietnam over the Spratlies, although Hanoi would definitely make every effort to involve Moscow. But the presence of a number of Soviet warships in the area would certainly complicate the entire situation and make any incident extremely volatile. Whatever the foreseeable future may hold, it is quite clear that neither the Sino-Vietnamese land border nor the vast South China Sea will see peace and tranquility for a long time to come.

Notes

1. The Chinese version of these conventions and related documents on the process and problems of negotiation were collected in the seven-volume *Zhong Fa zhanzheng* (The Sino-French War) (Shanghai: Renmin chuban she, 1961), particularly vol. 7, pp. 432–467. The French texts may be found in *Treaties between China and Foreign States*, vol. 1 (Shanghai: Published by order of the inspector general of Customs, 1908). Other related files are contained in Ministère des Affaires étrangères, *Documents diplomatique français, 1871–1940*, vols. 2–5, Ire serie (1871–1900).

2. In the 1880s, "9 out of every 10" residents of the border areas were reported to be ethnic Chinese, so that specific conventions had to be concluded to regulate the status and activities of these people, including freedom of movement across the border. See *Zhong Fa zhanzheng* vol. 7, pp. 434–439. Also, *Far Eastern Economic Review (FEER)* (May 5, 1978), 10; (September 1, 1978), 8–9.

3. See *Chingji waijiao shiliao* (Historical Documents of the Ching Dynasty Relating to Foreign Affairs) (Taipei: Wenhai chubanshe, 1963), particularly vols. 63, 67, and 68. *Zhong Fa Yuenan jiaoshe dang* (Official Files on the Sino-French Negotiations Concerning Vietnam) (Taipei: Academia Sinica, 1962), particularly pp. 4592–4645.

4. Beijing declared in 1979, "We made no attempt to change the state of jurisdiction even in those areas that clearly belonged to China according to the provisions of the Sino-French boundary

accords but which had been under Vietnamese jurisdiction for many years." Such was the situation "left over from history and prevailing in the early days following the liberation of China," *Beijing Review* (*BR*) (May 25, 1979), 15–16.

5. Vietnam thus claimed that after 1949, China had "borrowed"certain Vietnamese territories and incorporated certain Vietnamese villages into Chinese administrative units. See Vietnam's *Memorandum on the Sino-Vietnamese Border Conflict, March 15, 1979* (hereafter cited as *Memo.*), in British Broadcasting Corporation, *Summary of World Broadcasts*, Part III, Far East (*BBC/FE*) no. 6070 (March 19, 1979), C/1–13.

6. *Memo.*, C/2–3.

7. In one place, the dispute is over an area of less than one square kilometer (*FEER*, March 16, 1979), 10; *BR* (May 25, 1979), 20.

8. Both the French and the Chinese texts are contained in *Treaties between China and Foreign States*, vol. 1, p. 722. Also, *Vietnam Courier* (Hanoi), March 1979, p. 9; *BR* (May 25, 1979), 16.

9. Gulfs with an opening narrower than 24 miles are considered the inland sea of the coastal state. The largest "historical gulf" recognized internationally today is the Hudson Bay with an opening of about 80 miles. The Gulf of Tonkin has an open south end of 150 miles.

10. Offshore oil reserves in the South China Sea have been estimated to be in the neighborhood of three to eight billion barrels. See Selig S. Harrison, "Time Bomb in East Asia," *Foreign Policy* (Fall 1975), 6. Corazon Morales Siddayao, *The Off-Shore Petroleum Resources of Southeast Asia* (Kuala Lumpur: Oxford University Press, 1978), 26. Also by the same author, *Survey of Petroleum Reserves in Southeast Asia* (Kuala Lumpur: Oxford University Press, 1980), 17–20.

11. See Martin H. Katchen, "The Spratly Islands and the Law of the Sea: 'Dangerous Ground' for Asian Peace," *Asian Survey* (December 1977), 1170–1175; *FEER* (August 1981), 25.

12. A. Saix Olivier, "Iles Paracels," *La Geographie*, vol. 50, nos. 5 and 6 (November–December 1933): 240–241. Also see J. W. Reed and J. W. King, *The China Sea Directory* (London: The Hydrographic Office, the Admiralty, 1868).

13. *Zhonghua mingguo nanhai si da chundao jielue* (A Concise Account of China's Four Archipelagoes in the South China Sea) (Taipei: Ministry of Internal Affairs, 1948). See also, *FEER* (January 28, 1974), 9; (February 25, 1974), 25–28.

14. Olivier, "Iles Paracels." Also, *BBC/FE*, no. 6234 (October 2, 1979), A3/3; Chiu Hungda, *Guanyu Zhongguo lingtu de guoji fa wenti* (China's Territorial Problems in the Context of International Law) (Taipei: Shangwu yingshu guan, 1975), 221–223.

15. Ibid.

16. *Waijiao bu gongbao* (Communiqué of the Foreign Ministry) (Nanjing), vol. 6, no.3 (July–September 1933), 2. Also, Chiu, *Guanyu Zhongguo lingtu de guoji fa wenti*, pp. 202–210, 221–223.

17. *Waijiao bu zhoubao* (Weekly News of the Foreign Ministry) (Nanjing), November 11, 1946.

18. For a detailed account of these events, see *Lianhe Bao* (United Daily) (Taipei), February 25, 1974, p. 4.

19. Zhang Dajun, "Zhong-Yue guojie yu nanhai jiang yenjiu" (A Study of the Southern Section of the Sino-Vietnamese Border), *Bulletin of the Sun Yat-sen Cultural Foundation* (Taipei), no. 22 (November 1978): 625. Also, *BBC/FE*, no. 6234 (October 2, 1979), A3/8; no. 6932 (January 20, 1982), A3/7.

20. Zeng Zhaoxuan et al., *Meili fushu de nanhai zhudao* (The Beautiful and Resource-Rich Islands in the South China Sea) (Beijing: Shangwu yingshu guan, 1981), 91.

21. *Renmin Ribao* (People's Daily) (Beijing), August 16, 1951, p. 1. Also, *BR* (April 5, 1974), 8.

22. *Vietnam Courier*, February 1979, p. 11.

23. For an intensive analysis of the legal aspect of the subject, see Hungdah Chiu, "The Legal Status of the Paracel and Spratly Islands," *Ocean Development and International Law*, vol. 3, no. 1 (Spring 1975): 1–15. Also, Martin H. Katchen, "The Spratly Islands and the Law of the Sea," *Asian Survey* (December 1977): 1167–1181.

24. *The Straits Times* (Singapore) (*ST*), September 6, 1979, p. 5; *FEER* (April 28, 1983), 38.

25. For a detailed account of these events, see Lee Lai-to, "The PRC and the South China Sea," *Current Scene*, vol. 15, no. 2 (February 1977): 8–11.

26. *BR* (May 25, 1979), 14–16; *Memo.*, C/4.

27. Vietnam even set up and maintained schools, hospitals, and radio stations in China. *BR* (May 4, 1979), 11.

28. Mao said this on December 19, 1967. *BR* (December 25, 1967), 5.

29. *BR* (May 25, 1979), 15.

30. *FEER* (May 5, 1978), 11.

31. *BR* (March 30, 1979), 20. Also, *FEER* (March 16, 1979), 11.

32. *BR* (June 19, 1958), 21; *BR* (August 24, 1979), 25. The existence of such a statement and its contents were acknowledged by Vietnam in *BBC/FE*, no. 6189 (August 9, 1979), 1.

33. Ibid.; *BR* (August 24, 1979), 24. See also, *Nhan Dan* (Hanoi), May 10, 1965.

34. *BR* (May 25, 1979), 15–16; *Memo.*, C/2–3.

35. *BR* (May 25, 1979), 15.

36. Ibid.

37. Ibid.; *Memo.*, C/2.

38. Ibid.; *BR* (May 25, 1979), 15.

39. *Renmin Ribao*, February 27, 1959, p. 1; *BR* (April 9, 1959), 18–19.

40. *The Economist* (October 27, 1973), 63; Lee, "PRC and South China Sea," 9; *BBC/FE*, no. 6234, p. A3/8.

41. Lee, "PRC and South China Sea," 8. Also, *BBC/FE*, no. 6234, p. A3/8.

42. *BBC/FE*, no. 4499 (February 22, 1974), A3/2; *FEER* (October 22, 1973), 27.

43. *Memo.*, 6; *BR* (December 29, 1978), 23.

44. *Memo.*, 6.

45. *China News Analysis* (March 15, 1974), 7. For an account of the clash, see Lee, "PRC and South China Sea," 7–8; *FEER* (January 28, 1974), 32.

46. See the Vietnam government's White Paper on the Paracels and Spratlies released on September 28, 1979, in *BBC/FE*, no. 6234, p. A3/8.

47. *BR* (December 29, 1978), 23; *Memo.*, C/6; *BBC/FE*, no. 6120 (May 19, 1979), A3/7.

48. *BR* (May 25, 1979), 16–17.

49. *Memo.*, C/6; *BBC/FE*, no. 6298 (December 15, 1979), A3/1.

50. *BR* (May 25, 1979), 16–17; *Memo.*, C/6.

51. *BR* (May 18, 1979), 16. *The Voice of the Nation* (Bangkok), November 23, 1974.

52. According to Radio Hanoi, the following islands were "liberated": Song Tu Tay (Southwest Cay), Son Ca (Sand Cay), Nam Yet (Nam Yit), Sinh Ton (Sin Cowe), Truong Sa (Spratly Island), An Bang (Amboyana Cay). *The Monitoring Digest* (Singapore) *MD* (May 7, 1975), 8. See Map 2.

53. *BR* (May 25, 1979), 26.

54. *FEER* (May 28, 1976), 113–115.

55. *South China Morning Post* (Hong Kong), July 16, 1976.

56. *Renmin Ribao*, September 18, 1975.

57. The two sides recognized that differences of view existed and agreed to hold further talks in the future. *BR* (August 24, 1979), 26. Also, *BBC/FE*, no. 6189, p. A3/1.

58. Lee, "PRC and the South China Sea," 9–10.

59. Ibid., 10.

60. *FEER* (May 28, 1976), 13; (October 7, 1977), 86–87.

61. *BBC/FE*, no. 5228 (June 8, 1976), A3/3.

62. He also disclosed that the Sino-Vietnamese territorial dispute was "above all a dispute over the islands in the South China Sea," *BBC/FE*, no. 5254 (July 8, 1976), A3/1.

63. *BBC/FE*, no. 5266 (July 22, 1976), A3/1.

64. *Xinhua News Agency* (Beijing) (*XHNA*) (June 14, 1976).

65. *XHNA* (August 31, 1976).

66. *BBC/FE*, no. 6009 (January 6, 1979), A3/6; *Vietnam Courier*, February 1979, p. 12. Also, *BR* (May 25, 1979), 21.

67. *BR* (May 25, 1979), 20–21; *Memo.*, 3.

68. *BR* (May 25, 1979), 21–22.

69. *Memo.*, C/4.

70. *BR* (March 30, 1979), 19. According to Vietnam, the number was 197 in 1974. *Vietnam Courier*, March 1979, p. 8.

71. *BR* (March 30, 1979), 19.

72. Ibid.; Vietnam reported 294 cases of Chinese violations of Vietnamese territory in 1975, 812 in 1976, and 973 in 1977. *Vietnam Courier*, March 1979, p. 8.

73. *XHNA* (January 19, 1979).

74. *Vietnam Courier*, February 1979, p. 12.

75. *Memo.*, 7. *BR* (May 25, 1979), 22; (August 24, 1979), 26.

76. See Vietnam's explanation in *Memo.*, C/6. Also, *FEER* (May 7, 1976), 6–7.

77. See Li Xiannian's memorandum to Pham Van Dong in June 1977, reproduced in *BR* (March 30, 1979), 22.

78. *FEER* (October 3, 1975), 19–20. As early as November 1975, Moscow had accused China of laying claim to the Paracels, which "the Vietnamese consider to be their territory." *FEER* (December 12, 1975), 29. But around the same time, Vietnam still expressed the view, at least publicly, that the Sino-Soviet rift was not deep and would eventually disappear. *FEER* (November 14, 1975), 24.

79. *BR* (March 30, 1979), 22.

80. On November 15, 1976, the United States vetoed Viet-

nam's application to join the United Nations. In early 1977, the U.S.-Vietnam talks in Paris on normalization of relations ended in deadlock because of Vietnam's insistence on U.S. aid. *FEER* (May 13, 1977), 12–13. On the other hand, Moscow condemned China vehemently again in July 1976 for laying claims to Vietnamese territory in the South China Sea. *BBC/FE*, no. 5254, pp. A3/1–2.

81. The pro-Chinese faction in the leadership circles was purged at the Fourth Congress of the Vietnam Worker's Party held in December 1976. *FEER* (June 9, 1978), 11.

82. *BR* (May 25, 1979), 21. *XHNA* (January 19, 1979). Vietnam did not deny this charge made by China. See *BBC/FE*, no. 6022 (January 22, 1979), A3/5.

83. *BBC/FE*, no. 5518 (May 21, 1977), C/1.

84. *BR* (March 30, 1979), 21. Also, *FEER* (March 16, 1979), 11.

85. *BR* (March 30, 1979), 21. The same argument was repeated by Vietnam on August 7, 1979. See *BBC/FE*, no. 6189, p. A3/1.

86. *Memo.*, 7.

87. *BR* (May 25, 1979), 22.

88. *Memo.*, 7.

89. Ibid. Also, *BBC/FE*, no. 6120, p. A3/7.

90. Ibid., 9.

91. Ibid. Also, *Memo.*, 7; *BR* (May 25, 1979), 17.

92. *Memo.*, 7; *BR* (May 25, 1979), 17.

93. *BR* (May 4, 1979), 17.

94. *BR* (May 25, 1979), 18. Also, *BBC/FE*, no. 6120, pp. A3/7–8.

95. *BR* (May 25, 1979), 16.

96. Ibid., 17; *BBC/FE*, no. 6120, p. A3/6.

97. *Memo.*, 7; *BR* (May 25, 1979), 16–17.

98. *BR* (May 25, 1979), 17–18.

99. Ibid., 18. See also *Zhong Fa zhanzheng*, vol. 7, p. 453.

100. *BR* (May 25, 1979), 18; *BBC/FE*, no. 6120, p. A3/8.

101. *BBC/FE*, no. 6120, p. A3/10.

102. Ibid., A3/8–10. Also, *BBC/FE*, No. 6070, pp. C/12–13; no. 6095 (April 19, 1979), A3/4–5.

103. *BBC/FE*, no. 6095, pp. A3/4–5.

104. Ibid.; *BR* (May 25, 1979), 18.

105. Beijing charged, and Hanoi did not deny, that the talks were unilaterally suspended by Vietnam on the pretext that it was "too busy to negotiate." *BR* (May 25, 1979), 22.

106. See *FEER* (May 5, 1978), 10–11; (September 1, 1978), 8–9.

107. *BR* (August 18, 1977), 28. Also, *FEER* (May 5, 1978), 10.

108. As early as October 1977, Vietnam reportedly had already begun to expel Chinese residents in the border provinces into China, and this was followed by the fortification of some border towns in preparation for a possible showdown of force. *BR* (June 16, 1978), 15; (August 18, 1978), 29.

109. See Pao-min Chang, *Beijing, Hanoi, and the Overseas Chinese* (Berkeley, Calif.: Institute of East Asian Studies, 1982), 23–24.

110. It is perhaps noteworthy that in the Vietnam-Kampuchea border dispute Hanoi took the position that Vietnam's wartime pledges to respect the existing borders of Kampuchea had been made under the pressure of war against U.S. imperialism and that the pre-1954 French maps of Indochina delineated only the "administrative and police" jurisdiction of Cochin China and Kampuchea, leaving the question of their territorial sovereignty unsettled. *Vietnam Courier*, February 1978, p. 6. *Vietnam* (Hanoi), June 1978, p. 3. Also, *BR* (July 21, 1978), 6. Hanoi's stances on the two territorial disputes therefore appear to reinforce each other, and presumably any concession made on either one would weaken its position on the other.

111. In early January of 1979, China released the full text of the Kampuchean statement on the Vietnam-Kampuchea conflict but only excerpts of the Vietnamese statement. *BR* (January 6, 1978), 3. *ST*, January 10, 1978, p. 1; January 14, 1978, p. 5.

112. Chang, *Beijing, Hanoi, and the Overseas Chinese*, 25–28.

113. *BR* (June 16, 1978), 17.

114. *BR* (July 21, 1978), 24.

115. *XHNA* (August 25, 1978). Vietnam claimed that it was the Chinese who were trying to send spies and saboteurs into Vietnam. Vietnam also reported 2 Vietnamese killed and 25 wounded. *BBC/FE*, no. 6902 (August 29, 1978), A3/2.

116. Vietnam did not deny the occupation. *ST*, August 29, 1978, p. 1; August 30, 1978, p. 1; September 5, 1978, p. 22; September 6, 1978, p. 24. Also, *FEER* (September 8, 1978), 10. About the same time, Hanoi also reported the seizure of six Chinese fishing boats in the Gulf of Tonkin that had allegedly intruded into its territorial waters. *ST*, August 30, 1978, p. 1.

117. For instance, *XHNA* (September 18, November 15 and 27, 1978).

118. For instance, *Radio Hanoi*, December 5, 1978. See also November 1 and 17, 1978; December 15 and 22, 1978. *ST*, September 26, 1978, p. 1; October 13, 1978, p. 5; November 4, 1978, p. 32.

119. *XHNA* (December 21 and 24, 1978); *BR* (December 29, 1978), 22.

120. Calculated from data contained in *Vietnam Courier*, November 1978, p. 3; *BBC/FE*, no. 5985 (December 4, 1978), A3/5; no. 5996 (December 16, 1978), A3/3.

121. *XHNA* (December 22, 1978); *BBC/FE*, no. 6022 (January 22, 1979), A3/5.

122. After the conclusion of the Vietnamese-Soviet Treaty of Friendship and Cooperation, Deng Xiaoping said that China's reaction "would depend upon the moves by Vietnam. . . . First we must watch how much aggression they make against Kampuchea. Then we will decide about measures that we will take." *ST*, November 9, 1978, p. 28.

123. See Chang, *Beijing, Hanoi, and the Overseas Chinese*, 46; Chang, *Kampuchea Between China and Vietnam*, 80–82.

124. *BR* (March 2, 1979), 23–25; *Memo.*, 10–11.

125. For instance, *XHNA* (September 18, November 15, November 27, and December 9, 11, 13, and 20, 1978); (January 4, 1979). *BBC/FE*, no. 5969 (November 15, 1978), A3/4; no. 5997 (December 18, 1978), A3/9; no. 6001 (December 22, 1978), A3/2.

126. See Han Nianlong's speech at the second meeting of the Sino-Vietnamese talks carried in *XHNA* (April 26, 1979). As late as early January 1979, Japanese journalist Shuzo Aoki, who had made a field trip to the Sino-Vietnamese border, reported "From the state of affairs one finds in Youyiguan and Dongxing [which had been the scene of more than 100 armed incidents], one may draw this conclusion: At least for the present the Vietnamese side is making incessant provocations while the Chinese side is exercising great restraint. But this restraint is approaching its limit," *Tokyo Shimbun* (Tokyo), January 1, 1979.

127. *Radio Hanoi*, November 1–3, 1978; *Vietnamese News Agency*, November 1–3, 1978; *XHNA* (November 7, 1978).

128. Another 40 thousand Chinese were driven across the land border in the last five months of 1978, including nearly 10 thousand in December alone. *XHNA* (December 10, 1978, January 5, 1979).

129. *XHNA* (January 5, 1979).

130. *XHNA* (December 14, 24, 27, and 28, 1978). Also, *ST*,

December 15, 1978, p. 6. It is noteworthy that Vietnam did not accuse China of similar acts until late January. *Memo.*, 10–11.

131. *XHNA* (December 10, 1978); *BR* (December 22, 1978), 13. Vietnam did not deny the charges but claimed that Chinese vessels had intruded into Vietnamese waters. *BBC/FE*, no. 5992 (December 12, 1978), A3/3. See also, *FEER* (December 22, 1978), 17.

132. *BBC/FE*, no. 6009, p. A3/6.

133. *BBC/FE*, no. 6005 (January 1, 1979), A3/1.

134. *Vietnam Courier*, February 1979, p. 10.

135. *BR* (February 23, 1979), 8.

136. *XHNA* (December 12, 13, 24, and 25, 1978); *BR* (December 22, 1978), 14 and (December 29, 1978), 24–25. Also, *XHNA* (January 19 and February 11, 1979).

137. *XHNA* (December 24, 1978).

138. Ibid., 25. Also, *BR* (December 29, 1978), 24–25.

139. The phrase was first used on January 8. See *ST*, May 4, 1979, p. 16. Deng Xiaoping repeated it on January 31, 1979 in the United States and again on February 6, in Tokyo on his way back to Beijing. *New York Times*, February 1, 1979, p. 1 and February 7, 1979, p. 3. Also, *XHNA* (February 11 and 17, 1979). It was cited again by China after launching the invasion of Vietnam. *ST*, February 28, 1979, p. 1.

140. *ST*, January 7, 1979, p. 2; January 23, 1979, p. 2; February 19, 1979, p. 12. For a detailed account of the war, see King C. Chen, *China's War against Vietnam, 1979: A Military Analysis* (Baltimore, Md.: University of Maryland Law School, 1983).

141. *BR* (December 29, 1978), 25. *ST*, January 23, 1979, p. 2.

142. *BBC/FE*, no. 6047 (February 20, 1979), A3/10; *BR* (May 25, 1979), 21.

143. Deng Xiaoping said in late February that China was prepared for a possible war with the Soviet Union. *ST*, February 28, 1979, p.1.

144. *XHNA* (February 17, 1979). Also, *ST*, February 28, 1979, p. 1.

145. *ST*, February 20, 1979, p. 26 and March 10, 1979, p. 1. See also Vietnam's account of China's war crimes in *BBC/FE*, no. 6095 (April 19, 1979), A3/2.

146. *FEER* (March 9, 1979), 13–14. Also, Harlan W. Jencks, "China's 'Punitive' War on Vietnam: A Military Assessment," *Asian Survey* (August 1979): 809–810.

147. *XHNA* (February 17, 1979).

148. *XHNA* (February 17 and 26); (March 1 and 5, 1979). *ST*, February 26, 1979, p. 1 and March 4, 1979, p. 1.

149. *XHNA* (February 17; March 1, 6, 20, and 27, 1979).

150. *FEER* (March 16, 1979), 10–11.

151. *BBC/FE*, no. 6095, pp. A3/4–5.

152. Ibid.

153. *XHNA* (April 27, 1979).

154. *BBC/FE*, no. 6110 (May 5, 1979), A3/5.

155. *BBC/FE*, no. 6102 (April 27, 1979), A3/11; no. 6120, p. A3/6; no. 6155 (June 30, 1979), A3/3, 5; no. 6172 (July 20, 1979), A3/3.

156. *XHNA* (April 26, June 28, and July 18, 1979). Also, *BBC/FE*, no. 6121 (May 21, 1979), A3/4.

157. *BBC/FE*, no. 6102, p. A3/9; no. 6155, p. A3/4.

158. See for instance, *BBC/FE*, no. 6155, p. A3/4; no. 6157 (July 3, 1979), A3/9; no. 6189, p. A3/1; no. 6197 (August 18, 1979), A3/4.

159. *BBC/FE*, no. 6161 (July 7, 1979), A3/2; no. 6298, p. A3/1.

160. See for instance, *XHNA* (May 18, June 28, June 29, and July 28, 1979).

161. *XHNA*, (June 29 and July 5, 1979).

162. *XHNA* (August 14, 1979).

163. *BBC/FE*, no. 6189, p. A3/1; *Vietnam Courier*, November 1979, p. 7.

164. *BBC/FE*, no. 6194 (August 15, 1979), A3/11–12.

165. Ibid., 11.

166. *Vietnam Courier*, September 1979, p. 7.

167. Ibid.

168. Ibid., 13.

169. *BBC/FE*, no. 6232 (September 29, 1979), A3/1.

170. *BBC/FE*, no. 6234, pp. A3/1–9. See also *Vietnam Courier*, November 1979, pp. 6–7.

171. *BR* (February 18, 1980), 15–22.

172. Ibid., 15. The argument was repeated two years later: *BR* (July 12, 1982), 13–14.

173. *BR* (February 18, 1980), 21–22.

174. *Renmin Ribao*, April 7, 1980, p. 4.

175. *BR* (February 18, 1980), 22–24. *Renmin Ribao*, April 7, 1980, p. 4; August 1, 1980, p. 1.

176. *Renmin Ribao*, August 1, 1980, p. 1. Also in *BBC/FE*, no. 6494 (August 11, 1980), A3/2–5.

177. *Guangming Ribao* (Glorious Daily) (Beijing), April 5, 1980, p. 1. Also in *BBC/FE*, no. 6417 (May 12, 1980), A3/10.

178. *Guangming Ribao*, April 5, 1980, p. 1; *BR* (February 18, 1980), 23–24; *Renmin Ribao*, April 7, 1980, p. 1 and August 1, 1980, p. 1.

179. *Guangming Ribao*, December 2, 1980; in *BBC/FE*, no. 6617 (January 8, 1981), A3/1–7.

180. *BBC/FE*, no. 6617, pp. A3/1–7.

181. Ibid.

182. Ibid.

183. *BBC/FE*, no. 6932 (January 20, 1982), A3/1–15.

184. Ibid., A3/2–7.

185. Ibid., A3/8–9.

186. Ibid., A3/6–9.

187. Ibid., A3/12–13.

188. Ibid. Also, *BBC/FE*, no. 7087 (July 26, 1982), A3/10–11.

189. *BBC/FE*, no. 6932, A3/14–15.

190. Ibid.

191. Ibid., A3/12–13.

192. Ibid., A3/14–15.

193. Ibid. See also *BBC/FE*, no. 7087, pp. A3/10–12.

194. *Nhan Dan* (May 12, 1982).

195. Ibid.

196. Ibid.

197. *XHNA* (June 11, 1982).

198. Ibid.

199. Ibid.

200. Ibid.

201. *Radio Peking*, September 6, 1979; in *BBC/FE*, no. 6232, p. A3/2. *Radio Peking*, August 2, 1980; in *BBC/FE*, no. 6494, p. A3/6.

202. *XHNA* (July 23, 1979). Also, *BBC/FE*, no. 6212 (September 6, 1979), A3/2; *ST*, October 20, 1979, p. 3; October 24, 1979, p. 2.

203. *ST*, September 30, 1979, p. 1; October 17, 1979, p. 16.

204. *BBC/FE*, no. 6235 (October 3, 1979), A3/7. A ferry service between Hainan and the Paracels involving a 2,000-ton passenger-cargo ship was inaugurated in late December of 1978. *XHNA* (December 26, 1978).

205. *Radio Peking*, August 2, 1980; in *BBC/FE*, no. 6494, p. A3/6.

206. *XHNA* (July 24 and 30, 1981).

207. *Radio Hanoi*, October 16, 1981; in *BBC/FE*, no. 6858 (October 20, 1981), A3/4.

208. *Renmin Ribao*, February 12, 1982, p. 1.

209. *ST*, June 26, 1982, p. 7.

210. In November, a Hong Kong fishing boat seeking asylum from a typhoon in the Paracels was fired at, resulting in the death of two fishermen. The *Hong Kong Standard*, November 22, 1982.

211. *Radio Peking*, February 8, 1983.

212. *ST*, September 30, 1979, p. 1; October 17, 1979, p. 16. *Petroleum News* (January 1980), 17–18.

213. *ST*, September 30, 1979, p. 1; *Petroleum News* (January 1982), 12.

214. *Petroleum News* (December 1980), Supplement and (January 1982), 13.

215. *XHNA* (September 26, 1979).

216. *ST*, July 27, 1980; *BR*, (September 26, 1983), 3; *ST*, October 5, 1983, p. 16; *XHNA* (September 29, 1982).

217. *Petroleum News* (May 1982), Supplement; *XHNA* (February 16, March 16, and April 26, 1982).

218. *ST*, September 27, 1982, p. 40; *Petroleum News* (January 1983), 12.

219. *XHNA* (April 24, 1983).

220. *BR* (September 26, 1983), 3; *ST*, October 5, 1983, p. 16.

221. *XHNA* (May 25, 1984).

222. *ST*, April 28, 1979, p. 3; May 14, 1979, p. 1.

223. *Radio Hanoi*, June 2, 1980; in *BBC/FE*, no. 6438 (June 6, 1980), A3/8; no. 6578 (November 18, 1980), A3/4.

224. *BBC/FE*, no. 6729 (May 21, 1981), A3/12.

225. *Radio Hanoi*, August 27, 1981; in *BBC/FE*, no. 6815 (August 31, 1981), A3/4. Unfortunately, it is not possible to identify these two islands yet. But because they were not among those already known to be under Vietnamese occupation, they must have been newly acquired by Hanoi.

226. *BBC/FE*, no. 6946 (February 5, 1982), A2/1.

227. Ibid.; *BBC/FE*, no. 6956 (February 17, 1982), A2/1.

228. *ST*, October 28, 1982.

229. There have been frequent reports on refugee boats being shot at and sunk near the Vietnam-occupied islands. For instance, *XHNA* (May 29, 1978); *ST*, June 29, 1979, p. 2. As late as April 1983, a German pleasure boat was sunk near Amboyana Island. *FEER* (April 28, 1983), 39.

230. The six islands are Person Reef, Eldad Reef, Union Banks and Reefs, Central Reef, Owen Shoal, Rifleman Bank. Ibid., 38; *ST*, May 23, 1983, p. 1.

231. *ST*, May 24, 1984, pp. 3, 18; June 15, 1984, p. 3.

232. *Petroleum News* (January 1980), 60.

233. *ST*, May 15, 1980, p. 30.

234. *BBC/FE*, no. 6481 (July 26, 1980), A3/1.

235. *ST*, December 25, 1981, p. 3; *Petroleum News* (January 1982), 46.

236. *BBC/FE*, no. 6211 (September 5, 1979), A3/1; no. 6215 (September 10, 1979), A3/1.

237. *BBC/FE*, no. 6232, p. A3/1. Also, *ST*, October 17, 1979, p. 16; *BBC/FE*, no. 6298, p. A3/1.

238. *BBC/FE*, no. 6313 (January 11, 1980), A3/1.

239. *XHNA* (April 26, 1982); *Nhan Dan*, May 12, 1982, p. 3; *Petroleum News* (May 1982), Supplement; (January 1983), 54.

240. *ST*, September 27, 1982, p. 40. See also, *BBC/FE*, no. 7257 (February 14, 1983), A3/3.

241. *Petroleum News* (March 1983), 12.

242. *BBC/FE*, no. 7183 (November 15, 1982), A3/1.

243. *BBC/FE*, no. 7257, p. A3/3.

244. *BBC/FE*, no. 7685 (June 1, 1984), A3/4; no. 7660 (June 4, 1984), A3/6.

245. Revealed by *Radio Peking*, August 1, 1980; in *BBC/FE*, no. 6494, p. A3/6.

246. *ST*, October 17, 1979, p. 16.

247. *BBC/FE*, no. 6894 (December 1, 1981), A3/3.

248. *XHNA* (March 8, 1982). Vietnam corroborated the Chinese charge by reporting sea clashes between Vietnamese trawlers and a fleet of 40 Chinese armed vessels intruding into Vietnamese waters. It also admitted setting three of them ablaze. *BBC/FE*, no. 6971 (March 6, 1982), A3/3; *ST*, March 5, 1982, p. 1; March 9, 1982, p. 1; March 10, 1982, p. 4.

249. *XHNA* (March 10, 1982).

250. *XHNA* (June 2, 1982).

251. *XHNA* (July 26, 1982).

252. *BR* (October 24, 1983), 8.

253. Ibid.

254. *ST*, April 18, 1984, p. 4.

255. *Reuter Dispatch*, Jakarta, May 12, 1984; *ST*, May 24, 1984, pp. 3 and 18; *FEER* (June 14, 1984), 47.

256. *ST*, May 24, 1984, pp. 3 and 18; *FEER* (June 14, 1984), 47.

257. *ST*, May 3, 1979, p. 1.

258. *ST*, July 10, 1979, p. 26; October 8, 1979, p. 1; October 26, 1979, p. 1; April 16, 1981, p. 34; *New York Times*, December 8, 1979, p. 3; *XHNA* (April 21, 1980).

259. *Renmin Ribao*, July 23, 1979, p. 4; *ST*, October 6, 1980, p. 4.

260. *ST*, May 4, 1979, p. 1.

261. *ST*, August 8, 1979, p. 3.

262. *Vietnam Courier*, October 1979, p. 4; *BBC/FE*, no. 6280 (November 24, 1979), A3/1.

263. *BBC/FE*, no. 6652 (February 18, 1981), A3/2. For recent charges, see no. 7257, p. A3/3.

264. *XHNA* (November 20, 1979).

265. *ST*, July 7, 1980, p. 2. For more recent charges, see *XHNA* (July 13, 1981); (February 11, 1983).

266. *ST*, July 7, 1980, p. 2; November 13, 1980, p. 1.

267. *XHNA* (July 20, 1981); *BBC/FE*, no. 6786 (July 28, 1981), A3/10.

268. *ST*, February 9, 1982, p. 14.

269. See, for instance, *XHNA* (February 11 and 16, March 24, 1983). *BBC/FE*, no. 7076 (July 13, 1982), A3/6; no. 7239 (January 24, 1983), A3/1; no. 7282 (March 15, 1983), A3/3; no. 7293 (March 28, 1983), A3/6.

270. *XHNA* (April 10, 1983); *BBC/FE*, no. 7299 (April 5, 1983), A3/2.

271. *BR* (October 24, 1983), 8; *Renmin Ribao*, January 18, 1984, p. 8.

272. *XHNA* (March 28, 1984).

273. *BBC/FE*, no. 7609 (April 4, 1984), A3/10–11; no. 7613 (April 9, 1984), A3/1; no. 7616 (April 12, 1984), A3/1; no. 7619 (April 16, 1984), A3/4–5; no. 7627 (April 26, 1984), A3/1–2; no. 7630 (April 30, 1984), A3/2–3; no. 7635 (May 5, 1984), A3/5; no. 7636 (May 7, 1984), A3/9; no. 7642 (May 14, 1984), A3/9; no. 7646 (May 18, 1984), A3/2; no. 7652 (May 25, 1984), A3/1–3; no. 7659 (May 31, 1984), A3/1. *XHNA* (April 4, 7, 10, 12, 20, 29; May 1, 10, 16, 23; June 1, 1984).

274. *ST*, May 28, 1984, p. 32.

275. *ST*, July 14, 1984, p. 3.

276. China charged that Vietnam on November 18 and 19

alone fired more than 6,000 rounds of artillery shells into China's Malipo County in Yunnan Province, killing a number of people. *XHNA* (November 21, 1984). Vietnam also claimed that China fired thousands of artillery shells into Vietnam and made numerous armed incursions in mid-November. *BBC/FE*, no. 7801 (November 15, 1984), A3/1.

277. *Associated Press Dispatch*, Kunming, April 17, 1985.

278. According to Vietnam, "of the 170,000 Chinese enticed or coerced into leaving Vietnam for China by the Chinese side" in 1978, nearly 100 thousand came just from the border province of Quang Ninh. *Vietnam Courier*, March 1979, p. 8.

279. Although Soviet attacks on the links between China and overseas Chinese date back at least to 1970, they assumed new vigor only in July 1976. *Radio Peace and Progress*, July 6, 7, 14, in British Broadcasting Corporation, *Summary of World Broadcasts*, Part II, The Soviet Union, no. 5254 (July 8, 1976), A3/2; no. 5255 (July 9, 1976), A3/3; no. 5261 (July 16, 1976), A3/1–2; no. 5274 (July 31, 1976), A3/5. See also, Michael R. Godley, "Politics in the Penumbra: Chinese in Southeast Asia," *World Review* (April 1982), 75–83. Moscow expressed its sympathy for Vietnam in its territorial dispute with China only in November 1975 and came out openly in support of Vietnam in its conflict with Kampuchea only in January 1978. See *FEER* (December 12, 1975), 29; *Soviet News* (Singapore: The Soviet Embassy), January 10, 1978, pp. 1–4; February 14, 1978, pp. 11–14.

280. During the talks, Beijing went to great lengths to describe how China had helped Vietnam in material and human terms during the past 30 years. See *BR* (May 4, 1979), 10–11; (July 28, 1979), 27. Also, *XHNA* (July 30, 1979). Beijing claimed that as many as 300 thousand Chinese troops had gone to Vietnam between 1964 and 1971 to man antiaircraft guns and keep roads and railways open and supplies flowing. *ST*, July 31, 1979. p. 1.

281. See Zeng Zhaoxuan, *Meili fushu de nanhai zhudao*, pp. 90–91.

282. Apparently to bolster its presence in the South China Sea, in February 1982 the Taiwanese government approved a three-year plan for the development of the Pratas and the Sprat- lies, which included the construction of a large fishing port on Itu Aba and settlement of civilians. *Nanyang Siang Pow* (Singapore), February 8, 1982, p. 26. A survey ship was operating in the area by May of the same year. *Lianhe Bao* (United Daily) (Taipei), May

5, 1982. By late 1983, the Taiwanese had succeeded in growing dozens of kinds of vegetables and fruit trees on Itu Aba, thereby facilitating permanent settlement on the island. *Ta Kung Pao* (Hong Kong), November 23, 1983, p. 3. In early April 1984, a Bermuda yacht sailing past the Taiwan-occupied Pratas on its way to Hong Kong was fired upon by the troops stationed there, further demonstrating Taiwan's intention to defend its islands. *ST*, April 4, 1984, p. 4.

Appendix
The South China Sea Islands

English Name	Chinese Name	Vietnamese Name*
The Pratas	Dongsha Qundao	
Pratas Reef	Dongsha Jiao	
Pratas Island	Dongsha Dao	
North Verker Bank	Beiwei Tan	
South Verker Bank	Nanwei Tan	
North Channel	Bei Shuidao	
South Channel	Nan Shuidao	
The Paracels	Xisha Qundao	Quan Dao Hoang Sa
Crescent Group	Yongle Qundao	
North Reef	Bei Jiao	
Money Island	Jinyin Dao	Dao Vinh Lac
Antelope Reef	Lingyang Jiao	
	Kuangzai Shazhou	
Robert Island	Ganquan Dao	Dao Cam Tuyen
Pattle Island	Shanhu Dao	Dao Hoang Sa
	Quanfu Dao	
	Yagong Dao	

*Vietnam has yet to publish a complete list of Vietnamese names for these islands.

English Name	Chinese Name	Vietnamese Name
Observation Bank	Yin Yu	
	Yinyuzai	
	Xianshe Yu	
	Shi Yu	
Drummond Island	Jinqing Dao	Dao Duy Mong
Duncan Island	Chenhang Dao	Dao Quang Hoa
Palm Island	Guangjin Dao	
Vuladdore Reef	Yuzhuo Jiao	
Discovery Reef	Huaguang Jiao	
Passu Keah	Panshi Yu	Dao Bach Quy
Amphitrite Group	Xuande Qundao	
Triton Island	Zhongjian Dao	Dao Tri Ton
Woody Island	Yongxing Dao	Dao Phu Lam
Rocky Island	Shi Dao	Dao Hon Da
	Qilian Yu	
	Dongxin Shazhou	
	Xixin Shazhou	
South Sand	Nan Shazhou	
Middle Sand	Zhong Shazhou	
North Sand	Bei Shazhou	
South Island	Nan Dao	Dao Nam
Middle Island	Zhong Dao	Dao Trung
North Island	Bei Dao	Dao Bac
Tree Island	Zhaoshu Dao	Dao Cu Moc
West Sand	Xi Shazhou	Dao Cay
Iltis Bank	Yinli Tan	
Lincoln Island	Dong Dao	Dao Linh Con
Dido Bank	Xidu Tan	
Pyramid Rocks	Gaojianshi	
Naptuna Banks	Beibianlang	
Bremen Bank	Binmei Tan	
Jehangire Bank	Zhanhan Tan	
Bombay Reef	Langhua Jiao	
Herald Bank	Songtao Tan	
	Laochumen	
	Quanfumen	
	Yinyumen	
	Shiyumen	

English Name	Chinese Name	Vietnamese Name
	Jinqingmen	
	Hungcaomen	
	Zhaoshumen	
	Ganquanmen	
Macclesfield Bank	Zhongsha Qundao	
Siamese Shoal	Ximen Ansha	
Bankok Shoal	Bengu Ansha	
Magpie Shoal	Meibin Ansha	
Carpenter Shoal	Luban Ansha	
Oliver Shoal	Zhongbei Ansha	
Pigmy Shoal	Biwei Ansha	
Engeria Bank	Yinji Tan	
Howard Shoal	Wuyong Ansha	
Learmonth Shoal	Jimeng Ansha	
Plover Shoal	Haijiu Ansha	
Addington Patch	Anding Lianjiao	
Smith Shoal	Meixi Ansha	
Bassett Shoal	Bude Ansha	
Balfour Shoal	Bofu Ansha	
Parry Shoal	Paibo Ansha	
Cawston Shoal	Guodian Ansha	
Penguin Bank	Paihong Tan	
Tancred Shoal	Taojing Ansha	
Combe Shoal	Kongpai Ansha	
Cathy Shoal	Huaxia Ansha	
Hardy Patches	Shitang Lianjiao	
Hand Shoal	Zhizhang Ansha	
Margesson Shoal	Nanfei Ansha	
Walker Shoal	Manbu Ansha	
Phillip's Shoal	Lexi Ansha	
Payne Shoal	Pingnan Ansha	
Scarborough Reef	Huangyan Dao (Minzhujiao)	
South Rock	Nanyan	
North Rock	Beiyan	
Truro Shoal	Xianfa Ansha	

English Name	Chinese Name	Vietnamese Name
Helen Shoal	Yitong Ansha	
Saint Esprit Shoal	Shenhu Ansha	
	Zhongnan Ansha	
The Spratlies	Nansha Qundao	Quan Dao Truong Sa
North Danger Reefs	Shuangzi Qunjiao	
	Gongshi Jiao	
Northeast Cay	Beizi Dao	Son Tu Dong
	Beiwai Shazhou	
Southwest Cay	Nanzi Dao	Son Tu Tay
	Nailuo Jiao	
	Dongnan Ansha	
	Dongbei Ansha	
	Beizi Ansha	
Trident Shoal	Yongdeng Ansha	
Lys Shoal	Lesi Ansha	
Thitu Reefs	Zhongye Qunjiao	
	Tiezhi Jiao	
	Meijiu Jiao	
Thitu Island	Zhongye Dao	Hon Thi Tu
	Tiexian Jiao	
Subi Reef	Zhubi Jiao	
Loaita Bank & Reefs	Daoming Qunjiao	
	Shuanghuang Shazhou	
Loaita Island	Nanyue Dao	Hon Loai Ta
Lankiam Cay	Yangxin Shazhou	
	Kugui Jiao	
	Chang Tan	
Menzies Reef	Mengzi Jiao	
Tizard Bank & Reefs	Zhenghe Qunjiao	
Itu Aba Island	Taiping Dao	Dao Thai Binh
Sand Cay	Dunqian Shazhou	Son Ca
Petley Reef	Bolan Jiao	
Eldad Reef	Anda Jio	
Namyit Island	Hongxiu Dao	Hon Nam Yet
Gaven Reefs	Nanxun Jiao	

English Name	Chinese Name	Vietnamese Name
Discovery Small Reef	Xiaoxian Jiao	
Discovery Great Reef	Daxian Jiao	
Western Reef (Flora Temple Reef)	Fulusi Jiao	
Cornwallis Reef	Kangle Jiao	
Union Bank & Reefs (Union Tablemount)	Jiuzhang Qunjiao	
Sin Cowe Island	Jinghong Dao	Sinh Ton
	Nanmen Jiao	
West Reef	Ximen Jiao	
East Reef	Dongmen Jiao	
	Anle Jiao	
	Changxian Jiao	
	Zhuquan Jiao	
	Niu'e Jiao	
	Ranqing Dongjiao	
	Ranqing Shazhou	
	Longxia Jiao	
	Bianshen Jiao	
	Zhangxi Jiao	
	Quyuan Jiao	
	Qiong Jiao	
	Chiqua Jiao	
	Guihan Jiao	
	Hua Jiao	
	Jiyang Jiao	
Fancy Wreck Shoal	Fan'ai Ansha	
Ganges Reef	Fubo Jiao	
Fiery Cross Reef (Northwest Investigator Reef)	Yongshu Jiao	
Dhaulle Shoal	Xiaoyao Ansha	
Irving Reef	Huo'ai Jiao	
West York Island	Xiyue Dao	Dao Ben Lac

English Name	Chinese Name	Vietnamese Name
Nanshan Island	Mahuan Dao	
Flat Island	Feixin Dao	
Third Thomas Shoal	Heping Ansha Huoxing Jiao	
Nares Bank	Dayuan Tan	
Jackson Atoll	Wufangwei Wufangxi Wufangnan Wufangbei Wufangtou Xunjiang Ansha	
Pennsylvania Reef	Dongpo Jiao	
Brown Bank	Zong Tan	
Southern Bank	Bao Tan Donghua Jiao Bin Jiao	
Amy Douglas Bank	Antang Tan Antang Jiao	
Iroquois Reef	Houteng Jiao	
Baker Reef	Gongzhen Jiao	
Reed Bank	Liyue Tan	
Marie Louise Bank	Xiongnan Jiao	
Pennsylvania North Reef	Yangming Jiao Liyue Nanjiao Zi Tan	
Lord Aukland Shoal	Elan Ansha	
Carnatic Shoal	Hongshi Ansha	
Fairie Queen Bank	Xianhou Tan	
Templer Bank	Zhongxiao Tan Yongshi Tan	
Sandy Shoal	Shenxian Ansha	
Seahorse Bank	Haima Tan	
Ganges North Reef	Beiheng Jiao	
Eldad Reef	Heng Jiao	
Pennsylvania South Reef (?)	Kongming Jiao	

English Name	Chinese Name	Vietnamese Name
Southampton Reefs	Sanjiao Jiao	
	Lusha Jiao	
Mischief Reef	Meiji Jiao	
Alicia Annie Reef	Xian'e Jiao	
First Thomas Shoal	Xinyi Jiao	
Investigator Northeast Shoal	Haikou Jiao	
Half Moon Shoal	Banyue Jiao	
Royal Captain Shoal	Jianzhang Jiao	
Second Thomas Shoal	Ren'ai Jiao	
Sabina Shoal	Xianbin Jiao	
	Zhongshan Jiao	
	Lixin Jiao	
	Niuchelun Jiao	
	Pian Jiao	
Bombay Shoal	Pengbo Ansha	
Director Reef	Zhixiang Jiao	
Glasgow Shoal	Nanle Ansha	
Northeast Shoal	Xiaowei Ansha	
North Viper Shoal	Duhu Ansha	
Viper Shoal	Baowei Ansha	
Commodore Reef	Siling Jiao	
	Shaung Jiao	
	Shilongyan	
	Yixingshi	
	Wumie Jiao	
Cay Marino	Yunuo Jiao	
Cornwallis South Reef	Nanhua Jiao	
Pearson Reef	Liumen Jiao	
	Shipanzai	
Bittern Reef	Bisheng Jiao	
Investigator Shoal	Yuya Ansha	
	Erjiao Jiao	
	Langkou Jiao	
	Xiantou Jiao	

English Name	Chinese Name	Vietnamese Name
Southwest Shoal	Jinwu Ansha	
	Puning Ansha	
	Boji Jiao	
Ardrasier Bank	Andu Tan	
Gloucester Breakers	Polang Jiao	
	Guangxing Jiao	
	Guangxingzai Jiao	
Ardasier Breakers	Xibo Jiao	
Marivelas Reef	Nanhai Jiao	
Barque Canada Reef	Bai Jiao	
Lizzie Weber Reef	Danzhushi	
	Niaoyudingshi	
Amboyna Cay	Anbo Shazhou	Hon An Bang
Stay Shoal	Yindun Ansha	
London Reefs	Yinqing Qunjiao	
Cuarteron Reef	Huayang Jiao	
East Reef	Dong Jiao	
Central Reef	Zhong Jiao	
West Reef	Xijiao	
Spratly Island	Nanwei Dao	Truong Sa
Ladd Reef	Riji Jiao	
	Kangtai Tan	
	Zhuying Tan	
Owen Shoal	Aoyuan Ansha	
Breakers	Suilang Ansha	
Riflemen Bank	Nanwei Tan	
Bombay Castle	Pengbobao	
	Changjun Ansha	
Kingston Shoal	Jindun Ansha	
Orleana Shoal	Aonan Ansha	
Prince of Wales Bank	Guangya Tan	
Alexandra Bank	Renjun Tan	
Grainger Bank	Lizhun Tan	
Prince Consort Bank	Xiwei Tan	
Vanguard Bank	Wan'an Tan	

English Name	Chinese Name	Vietnamese Name
Swallow Reef	Danwan Jiao	
Royal Charlotte Reef	Huanglu Jiao	
Louisa Reef	Nantong Jiao	
North Luconia Shoals	Beikang Ansha	
Friendship Shoal	Mengyi Ansha	
	Yijing Jiao	
	Haikang Ansha	
	Faxian Ansha	
	Kangxi Ansha	
	Bei'an Jiao	
Seahorse Breakers	Nan'an Jiao	
Hayes Reef	Nanping Jiao	
South Luconia Shoals	Nankang Ansha	
	Yinbo Ansha	
Stigant Reef	Hai'an Jiao	
	Qiongtai Jiao	
	Tanmen Jiao	
Herald Reef	Haining Jiao	
Stera Blanca	Chengping Jiao	
	Huanle Ansha	
James Shoal	Zengmu Ansha	
	Zhong Shuidao	
	Tiezhi Shuidao	
	Nanhua Shuidao	

The above list is compiled mainly on the basis of the following sources:

1. *South China Sea: Gulf of Thailand to Taiwan* (Washington, D.C.: Defense Mapping Agency Hydrographic Center, 1970), Map No. 550.
2. *South Vietnam: Official Standard Names* (Washington, D.C.: U.S. Army Topographic Command, May 1971), 331–337 and relevant maps.
3. *Lianho Bao* (United Daily) (Taipei), February 25, 1974.
4. *Ban Do Hang Tinh Viet-Nam Cong-Hoa* (Saigon: Nha Dia-Du Quoc-Gia Viet-Nam An-Hanh, 1971), Plates 33, 35.
5. Dieter Heinzig, *Disputed Islands in the South China Sea* (Wiesbaden: Otto Harrassowitz, 1976).
6. *Renmin Ribao* (People's Daily) (Beijing), April 25, 1983.
7. *Nanhai Zhudao* (The South China Sea Islands) (Beijing: Ditu chubanshe, 1983).